Contents

Acknowledgments

The Central Office of Information would like to thank the following organisations for their co-operation in compiling this book: the Office of Population Censuses and Surveys, the Home Office, The Scottish Office, the General Register Office for Scotland, the Welsh Office, the Northern Ireland Information Service, the Overseas Development Administration and the United Nations.

Cover Photograph Credit

COI Pictures/John Nelligan.

Population

London: H M S O

Researched and written by Publishing Services, Central Office of Information.

© Crown copyright 1995
Applications for reproduction should be made to HMSO.
First published 1995

ISBN 0 11 702007 9

HMSO publications are available from:

HMSO Publications Centre
(Mail, fax and telephone orders only)
PO Box 276, London SW8 5DT
Telephone orders 0171 873 9090
General enquiries 0171 873 0011
(queuing system in operation for both numbers)
Fax orders 0171 873 8200

HMSO Bookshops
49 High Holborn, London WC1V 6HB
(counter service only)
0171 873 0011   Fax 0171 831 1326
68–69 Bull Street, Birmingham B4 6AD
0121 236 9696 Fax 0121 236 9699
33 Wine Street, Bristol BS1 2BQ
0117 9264306   Fax 0117 9294515
9–21 Princess Street, Manchester M60 8AS
0161 834 7201   Fax 0161 833 0634
16 Arthur Street, Belfast BT1 4GD
01232 238451   Fax 01232 235401
71 Lothian Road, Edinburgh EH3 9AZ
0131 228 4181   Fax 0131 229 2734
The HMSO Oriel Bookshop
The Friary, Cardiff CF1 4AA
01222 395548   Fax 01222 384347

HMSO's Accredited Agents
(see Yellow Pages)

and through good booksellers

Introduction

In Britain,[1] the total population has increased relatively slowly over the past few decades. From just over 50 million in 1951, it has grown to an estimated 58 million in 1993, an annual growth rate of 0.35 per cent. Only a small increase is projected in the next few decades, with the population likely to reach some 62 million in 2031.

There have, though, been a number of major demographic changes in recent years. As in many industrialised countries, the population of Britain is an ageing one, with increasing numbers of people over retirement age (60 for females, 65 for males)[2] and growing numbers of the very elderly—those over 75 years of age.

There have also been significant changes in the characteristics of households and families and the processes influencing them. There has been a rapid growth in cohabitation, divorce, lone parenting and individuals living alone. This has occurred not only in Britain but across much of the Western world. These trends are an important aspect of the changing social fabric of Britain.

Britain has a relatively high density of population compared with other countries. In recent decades, population has been moving away from the cities and large industrial towns to the smaller towns and rural areas. There has also been a strong pattern of retired people moving, particularly to the coastal areas of southern

[1] The term 'Britain' is used informally in this book to refer to the United Kingdom of Great Britain and Northern Ireland. 'Great Britain' comprises England, Wales and Scotland.
[2] The Government plans to equalise the state pension age for men and women at 65, although it does not envisage this beginning to take effect until 2010.

England. While southern England has grown in terms of population, the level of population in the north has remained relatively constant.

One of the most significant social changes in Britain since the Second World War has been the settlement of substantial immigrant communities, mainly from former colonies in the Caribbean and the South Asian sub-continent. Britain is now a multiracial society, with a non-white ethnic minority population in Great Britain of just over 3 million—about 5.5 per cent of the total population—of whom nearly half were born in Britain.

Worldwide population is growing at about 1.7 per cent a year, representing an annual addition to the world's population of over 90 million. The total population is estimated by the United Nations (UN) at around 5,660 million, and is expected to exceed 6,000 million later in the 1990s, rising to nearly 8,500 million in 2025.

This book describes the trends in population and changes in some of the main demographic characteristics. A selection of international comparisons is included, particularly in relation to other member states of the European Union. Government views on some of the main population issues are outlined. A section on world population contains a brief description of the programme of action adopted at the United Nations Conference on Population and Development, held in Cairo in September 1994.

Where possible, statistics are given for the whole of Britain. However, these are not always available and statistics are then given for Great Britain or, sometimes, for England and Wales. Figures are normally given for the latest available year, although in some cases these are provisional figures and may be subject to revision.

Key Statistical Sources

The main sources of statistics are the Census of Population, regular statistical surveys (such as the General Household Survey) and administrative statistical sources, such as registrations of births, marriages and deaths.

Britain was one of the first countries in the world to conduct a Census of Population. It was first conducted in 1801 and has been conducted every ten years (with one exception, in 1941) ever since. Registration of births, marriages and deaths was introduced in England and Wales in 1837 and in Scotland in 1855.

Monitoring of demographic indicators and the provision of advice on population matters are carried out by the Office of Population Censuses and Surveys (OPCS), a government department, the General Register Office for Scotland and the General Register Office for Northern Ireland. OPCS also co-ordinates interdepartmental work on population. Subject to consultation, the Government proposes to merge OPCS with the Central Statistical Office from April 1996.

The Census of Population

The Census of Population is the most important count of population and households in Britain at national and local level. It is organised by the OPCS in England and Wales, the General Register Office for Scotland and the Census Office for Northern Ireland. The funding, timing and content of each Census have to be approved by Parliament. The last Census of Great Britain and

Northern Ireland was conducted on 21 April 1991. By law, all house-holders are required to complete the Census form, for each person present (or absent but usually resident) at their address on Census night. The Census also covers people present on Census night in communal establishments and non-permanent accommodation (including boats, caravans, camping and people sleeping rough).

The Census is conducted by dividing the country up into enumeration districts. These are small areas, averaging about 150 households in size. An enumerator is assigned to each enumeration district, with responsibility for the distribution and collection of forms.

The 1991 form contained 25 basic questions about individuals, housing, household characteristics and various economic characteristics (such as employment). A notable feature of the 1991 Census was that, for the first time, it contained a question on ethnic groups in Great Britain, but not in Northern Ireland.

The Census obtained a 98 per cent response in 1991. The accuracy of the response and the characteristics of the non-response are assessed through the Census Validation Survey conducted on a small sample basis shortly after the Census itself. This provides an important check on the reliability of the detailed characteristics, rather than the total count.

The Census produces aggregated statistics on a wide range of subjects. One feature is that it provides a wealth of information on a local (as against a national) level. Population and household counts are published in Census Reports at local authority district level, and provided on magnetic media for computer analysis at much more local level. Publication details of a selection of the national Census reports and reports on particular topics are given in Further Reading, p. 97. An article in the OPCS quarterly

Population Trends Winter 1994[3] illustrates some of the results available from the Census for particular topics such as marital status, household and family composition, economic activity, ethnic group, migration and the Welsh and Gaelic languages.

The Census figures are used as a major input in the rebasing of the annual series of population estimates.

National Surveys

Small sample national surveys conducted by OPCS provide more frequent and more detailed information about a wide range of characteristics of the population. The following are among the most important.

The General Household Survey

The General Household Survey (GHS) is an annual survey carried out by OPCS which aims to monitor changes in household characteristics, and their consumption of housing. It has been conducted annually since 1971. For 1993, interviews were carried out between April 1993 and March 1994. Interviews were obtained from about 19,000 people aged over 16 in just over 10,000 households. The GHS contains questions on population, housing, employment, education and health. In addition to the basic questions repeated every year, special questions may be asked in individual survey years. For example, the 1993 GHS provides detailed information on contraception.

The Labour Force Survey

This looks at trends in the labour market and has been conducted since 1973. Originally conducted biennially, it was then conducted

[3] No 78. HMSO, £8.35. ISBN 0 11 691583 8.

annually until 1992. Since then it has been conducted quarterly in Great Britain, with a sample size of 60,000 (supplemented by a parallel survey of 4,000 households in Northern Ireland). The survey covers population and household topics as well as those relating to employment. The findings are published in the *Labour Force Survey Quarterly Bulletin*.

International Passenger Survey

Statistics on migration to and from Britain are obtained from the International Passenger Survey. It samples around 200,000 international passengers at ports and airports each year.

Registration Statistics

There are a large number of processes which are registered or formally recorded and which are subject to careful statistical analysis and subsequent publication.

Civil registration of births, deaths, marriages and divorce is considered a reliable source of information. Apart from recording the event itself, supporting information is collected, including parental details at birth, age at and cause of death, and partner details at marriage and divorce.

Migration is the most complex demographic process to measure adequately. The National Health Service Central Register provides statistics on migration between health authority areas in Britain. The statistics are produced from the administration of re-registrations of people with their General Practitioners. The area of the new registration and former registration can be used to quantify movements between locations and the age structure of the movers. It is not a perfect record, since it only deals with these non-compulsory registrations. However, it is regarded as a good approximation. As with the Census, it yields only partial information about international movements.

Intercensal Population Estimates

Population estimates are produced on an annual basis, for local authority and health authority areas. The estimates are published as a Mid-year Estimate Series (see Further Reading for statistics published by OPCS). The population estimation process draws heavily upon the registration of statistics described above.

Demographic Projections

The Government Actuary's Department prepares long-term national projections of population to 2061 and projections for England, Wales, Scotland and Northern Ireland to 2031. As well as total population, they also forecast age and gender composition, births, deaths and net migration. The Government Actuary's Department also prepares projections by marital composition. Population projections for local authority and health authority areas are prepared by OPCS, the General Register Office for Scotland and the General Register Office for Northern Ireland.

Statistical Digests

As well as the surveys and other reports referred to above, there are a number of official statistical publications which include information on population and related subjects. Among these are:

—*Population Trends*, a quarterly publication produced by OPCS, providing an up-to-date review of national demographic data and a time series over the preceding decades;

—*Regional Trends*, a Central Statistical Office (CSO) annual publication which includes a section on population and households, and which also has a table including population and population density for each region, county and district; and

—*Social Trends*, another CSO annual publication, with separate chapters on population and on households and families, with descriptions of the main trends.

Population Size and Density

The most recent estimate of Britain's population in 1993 indicates a total population of 58.2 million. This estimate is based on the 1991 Census of Population and relates to mid-year. In terms of population size, Britain ranks 17th in the world.

Britain has a relatively high population density of 241 people per square kilometre (sq km), which is well above the European Union (EU) average of 153 per sq km. England is the most densely populated country, with 372 people per sq km. Scotland has much the lowest population density, at 66 people per sq km. Northern Ireland and Wales have densities of 120 and 140 people per sq km respectively.

Historical Trends

It is believed that at the end of the 11th century the population of Britain was about 2 million. Population growth was held in check by relatively high death rates, particularly at childbirth and among young children. A lack of medical support and hygiene standards ensured that much of the population was vulnerable to malnutrition and disease, with famine a recurrent problem. Epidemics swept Europe from time to time. The most notorious was known as the Black Death, which reached Britain in 1348. It is suggested that up to one-third of the population was lost to this bubonic plague in the space of a few years. Population remained low for some time afterwards, but was rising again during the 16th century. By the end of the 17th century the population had risen to around 6.5 million, according to contemporary estimates.

Population records for the 19th century are more reliable than those for earlier centuries. Britain's first Census of Population in 1801 showed a population of over 10 million and painted a picture of a largely rural economy, with agriculture being the largest form of employment. However, the Industrial Revolution was already in progress and there had been a growth in urban population. The population of London had increased substantially in the 18th century and nearly 1 million people were living there in 1801. During the 19th century population expanded rapidly, doubling by 1851 to 20 million, and virtually doubling again by 1901. This reflected both higher fertility and greatly reduced death rates, thanks to improvements in public health, particularly drinking water supply, sanitation and medicine.

A major feature during the 19th century was the move to a more urbanised society. The Industrial Revolution was a significant factor in the growth of urban areas such as Glasgow, Birmingham, Leeds and Manchester. By the end of the century it was estimated that nearly 80 per cent of the population were living in urban districts with 10,000 or more people. Already in the second half of the century, however, the move away from the city centres to the suburbs had begun, facilitated by the growth of railways and tramways, which enabled people to travel longer distances into work.

Twentieth Century Trends

In Britain the 20th century has seen a rapid deceleration in population growth from the very high rates of the 19th century. Early in the 20th century, growth rates were still relatively high. During the decade 1901–1911, for example, the population grew by over

Table 1: Population

Thousands

	England	Wales	Scotland	Great Britain	Northern Ireland	United Kingdom
1901[a]	30,515	2,013	4,472	37,000	1,237	38,237
1931[a]	37,359	2,593	4,843	44,795	1,243	46,038
1961	43,561	2,635	5,184	51,380	1,427	52,807
1971	46,412	2,740	5,236	54,388	1,540	55,928
1981	46,821	2,813	5,180	54,814	1,538	56,352
1991	48,208	2,891	5,107	56,206	1,601	57,807
1992	48,378	2,899	5,111	56,388	1,618	58,006
1993	48,533	2,906	5,120	56,559	1,632	58,191
2031[b]	52,435	2,977	4,998	60,410	1,831	62,241

Sources: OPCS, General Register Offices for Scotland and Northern Ireland, and Government's Actuary Department.

[a] Populations enumerated in the Census. Figures for later years allow for Census under-recording.

[b] Mid-1992 based population projections.

10 per cent. However, over the period 1971–93 the population grew by only 4 per cent, reaching 58.2 million in 1993 (see Table 1).

There has however been a significant variation in the rates of recent change in population between the four constituent countries of Britain. Between 1971 and 1993 the highest rates of growth, 6 per cent, were experienced in Wales and Northern Ireland, while the rate of change in England was close to the national average. On the other hand, the population of Scotland fell by 2 per cent to 5.1 million.

Table 2 shows the average annual population changes experienced in Britain for various decades during the 20th century.

Annual growth exceeded 200,000 people for most decades until the 1970s. During the 1970s the growth rate was little more than 40,000 a year, although it then rose to 145,000 a year in the 1980s.

Three factors influence movements in overall levels of population: the 'natural changes' arise from births and deaths, and change also results from migration. There has been a substantial reduction in the birth rate, and large families are much less common than in the past. Age-specific death rates have continued to fall throughout the century, although the First and Second World Wars were the cause of over 1 million military and civilian deaths. This large loss of young men also had a significant effect on births by reducing the number of potential fathers; it is estimated that over half a million potential births did not take place as a result of these deaths. Throughout much of the 20th century, Britain has tended to lose population through emigration. Migration was particularly significant in the early decades of the century. More detailed information on births and deaths is given in the appropriate chapters.

Future Growth

According to the most recent official projections, working from a base of mid-1992, the slow rate of population growth experienced in recent decades is expected to continue (see Table 2). Britain's population is projected to rise to 59.8 million in 2001, 61.3 million in 2011 and 62.1 million in 2021. Thereafter there would only be a very small rise, to 62.2 million in 2031, and by that time deaths are forecast to exceed births.

Births are forecast to decline to below 700,000 a year by the 2030s. The official population projections also suggest that the

Table 2: Population Change

Thousands

	Population in Britain at start of period	Live births	Deaths	Net natural change	Net migra- tion and other change	Overall annual change
			Average Annual Change			
1901–11[a]	38,237	1,091	624	467	–82	385
1911–21[a]	42,082	975	689	286	–92	195
1921–31[a]	44,027	824	555	268	–67	201
1931–51[a]	46,038	793	603	190	22	213
1951–61	50,225	839	593	246	12	258
1961–71	52,807	962	638	324	–14	310
1971–81	55,928	736	666	69	–27	42
1981–91	56,352	757	655	103	43	146
1991–93	57,808	779	637	142	50	192
Mid-year projections[b]						
1993–2001	58,179	776	623	153	50	203
2001–11	59,800	716	614	102	44	146
2011–21	61,257	718	635	83	6	89
2021–31	62,146	703	693	9	0	9
2031–41	62,241	666	767	–102	0	–102
2041–51	61,223	656	819	–163	0	–163

Sources: OPCS, General Register Office for Scotland, General Register Office for Northern Ireland, Government Actuary's Department and *Social Trends*.
[a] Population figures for 1901–51 inclusive are as enumerated in censuses. Estimates for later years take account of under-recording in the Census.
[b] Projections based on 1992 estimates. The 1993 figure was subsequently revised to 58,191,000.
Note: Differences between totals and the sums of their component parts are due to rounding.

numbers of deaths will stay below 700,000 a year until the 2020s. They will then rise and by the 2040s are expected to exceed 800,000 a year. A notable feature of the official projections is that the population will continue to age. The dependency ratio (the number of dependants per 100 population of working age) is forecast to rise, particularly after 2021, from 63 in 1991 to reach 82 in 2036.

Looking at the constituent countries of Britain, official projections in the period to 2031 forecast a varying pattern. Northern Ireland is the only country where the population is forecast to increase throughout this period. The population of England is expected to rise for nearly all this period, but to peak around 2027 and then begin to fall. In Scotland the population is projected to rise until about 2000, but then to start falling, mainly as a result of the forecast loss of people through migration. For Wales the population is projected to rise to about 2015, but then to decline. By 2031 the population is forecast as 62.2 million for Britain: 52.4 million for England, just under 5 million for Scotland, nearly 3 million in Wales and over 1.8 million in Northern Ireland.

European Comparisons

Within the 12 countries of the European Union in 1994,[4] Britain accounts for about one-sixth of the population. Germany is the largest country in terms of population numbers, with some 80 million people (see Table 3) following unification. Britain, France and Italy are next in size, all with a similar level of population.

Britain is the third most densely populated country in the EU. The Netherlands has the greatest population density of the 12, with

[4] The European Union increased to 15 member countries from the beginning of 1995, when Austria, Finland and Sweden joined the Union. Statistics in this publication relate to the 12 member states in 1994 unless otherwise stated.

a density similar to that of England. The North West region of England is one of the most densely populated regions in the EU. Scotland though has one of the lowest population densities, although higher than the Irish Republic, which is the least crowded of the 12 EU members with 51 people per sq km.

Britain has both an above average proportion of young people and an above average proportion of elderly people when compared with other EU member states. Among EU regions Northern Ireland has one of the highest proportions of young people, although this is below that of the Irish Republic (the EU country with the highest proportion of young people). South West England has the joint second highest percentage of elderly people in the population, with the Centro region of Italy, and is exceeded only by the neighbouring Italian region of Emilia-Romagna.

Births and fertility rates have been falling throughout the EU. Britain however has the second highest birth rate of the 12 states. Northern Ireland's birth rate is the highest of any EU region.

The crude death rate in Britain is above the EU average, reflecting the greater than average number of elderly people. Britain has the highest death rate arising from circulatory diseases and the second biggest rate of deaths from cancer. However, it shares with the Netherlands the lowest rate of deaths from road accidents.

Where appropriate, further information on European comparisons is given in the following chapters, and Table 15 on p. 85 gives a selection of world population indicators.

Government Policy

The Government's views on population issues were set out in a statement issued in connection with the European Population

Table 3: European Union Comparisons (1991)

	Population (thousands)	People per sq km	% aged under 15	% aged 65 or over	Birth rate	Death rate
Belgium	10,005	328	18.1	15.0	12.5	10.4
Britain	57,790	237	19.1	15.7	13.7	11.1
Denmark	5,154	120	17.0	15.6	12.5	11.6
France	57,055	105	20.1	14.1	13.3	9.1
Germany	80,014	224	16.2	14.9	10.4	11.4
Greece	10,200	77	18.7	14.2	10.1	9.4
Irish Republic	3,524	51	26.9	11.4	15.0	8.9
Italy	56,760	188	16.5	15.1	9.8	9.6
Luxembourg	387	150	17.5	13.4	12.9	9.6
Netherlands	15,068	367	18.2	12.9	13.2	8.6
Portugal	9,862	107	20.0	13.6	11.8	10.5
Spain	39,025	77	19.4	13.5	10.1	8.6
European Union	344,843	146	18.2	14.6	11.6	10.1

Source: Statistical Office of the European Communities.

Notes:

(1) Figures for Britain may not be directly comparable to those used elsewhere in this book owing to different definitions.

(2) With the accession of Austria, Finland and Sweden to the EU in January 1995, the number of people in the EU has increased to around 366 million. Sweden has around 8.6 million people, Austria 8 million and Finland 5 million.

Conference 1993.[5] This says that the Government does not pursue a population policy in the sense of actively trying to influence the overall size of Britain's population, its age structure or the components of change except in the field of immigration. Its primary concern is for the well-being of the population, although it monitors

[5] A full text of Britain's statement was published in *Population Trends* Summer 1993 (No 72, HMSO, £8.15, ISBN 0 11 691538 2).

demographic trends and developments. It considers that decisions about fertility and childbearing should be made by individuals, but that people should be provided with the information and means necessary to make their decisions effective. Accordingly, the Government provides assistance with family planning as part of the National Health Service (NHS). Social and economic issues are raised by the growing proportions of elderly people, but the Government believes that these should prove manageable.

The Government takes population issues into account in formulating economic and social policy.

International Migration

The basic principles of government policy on immigration control are:

— to allow genuine visitors and students to enter Britain;

— to give effect to the free movement provisions of European Community law; and

— thereafter to restrict severely the numbers coming to live permanently or to work in Britain.

However, spouses and minor children of those already settled in Britain continue to be admitted in accordance with the Immigration Rules. The Government takes action to ensure that this policy is applied firmly and fairly.[6] There are no controls or restrictions on would-be emigrants from Britain.

---

[6] See pp. 29–33 for statistics on international migration. More information on immigration policy is given in *Immigration and Nationality* (Aspects of Britain: HMSO, 1993).

Family Issues

The Government regards the stability of the family and family relationships as important factors contributing to the well-being of the population. It does not consider that it is the role of government to intervene in family life, and it does not pursue policies designed to discourage divorce or cohabitation; however, it does try to ensure that, both within the family and where family breakdown has occurred, the welfare of any dependent children is of overriding priority. Accordingly, the Government seeks to ensure that when family breakdown has taken place, both parents should continue to provide for the maintenance of their children. To this end the Child Support Agency was established in April 1993 and over a four-year period is replacing the court system for obtaining maintenance for children.

Policies are formed with regard to the well-being of the population, such as on social, economic and environmental planning, rather than with regard to population size or growth. The Government regards family planning as an important health care service which contributes to maternal and child health and to the stability of family life. One matter of concern is the level of conceptions in those aged under 16, which has been increasing. The Government has set a target of reducing the rate of conceptions among the under 16s by at least 50 per cent by the year 2000.

Legislation places a duty on government, and hence health authorities, to ensure that a full range of contraceptive services, including sterilisation, is available. NHS family planning services are freely available to everyone. Guidance issued by the Government says that a choice of family planning advice should be available in every locality. It also asks health authorities to provide male and female sterilisation operations free of charge under the NHS for family planning purposes, as well as on medical grounds.

The Government 'maintains a neutral stance on abortion'. Legislation permits abortions in Great Britain (but not in Northern Ireland) if carried out in accordance with the criteria set out. Abortions are allowed to take place if two registered medical practitioners give a certified opinion in good faith that one or more of the specified conditions are met. Although Northern Ireland is excluded from the Abortion Act 1967, therapeutic terminations of pregnancy are carried out in Northern Ireland on medical grounds to preserve the life of the mother or to prevent serious damage to her physical or mental health.

Health

The Government's concern with the rates of morbidity and mortality led to the publication in 1992 of a strategy for improving the health of the population and reducing substantially the rates of morbidity and mortality (see Further Reading). Targets have been set in five key areas:

—coronary heart disease and strokes;

—cancers;

—mental illness;

—HIV/AIDS and sexual health; and

—accidents.

Most targets relate to the year 2000. A number of health promotion campaigns have been established in areas such as smoking and HIV/AIDS. For further information see p. 64.

International Co-operation

Population assistance to developing countries is a priority activity within the Government's overseas aid programme. The Government has three main principles for population activities in developing countries:

—individuals, particularly women, should be free and able to choose when to have children and to have means to act on these choices;

—reproductive choices should be fully informed, and not subject to pressure or coercion of any kind; and

—the quality and availability of family planning services must be improved if they are to win people's confidence.

Direct population assistance has grown substantially in recent years. About three-quarters of overseas aid spending on population activities in developing countries is on a multilateral basis, going to the United Nations Population Fund, the International Planned Parenthood Federation and the World Health Organisation Human Reproduction Programme.

Britain was one of 180 countries represented at the United Nations Conference on Population held in Cairo in September 1994. Information on the programme adopted at the Conference and on the British Government's views is given in the chapter on World Population (see pp. 84–91).

Population Distribution

In 1993 England had a population of 48.5 million, Scotland 5.1 million, Wales 2.9 million and Northern Ireland 1.6 million people.

For statistical purposes England is sub-divided into eight standard regions and their populations, together with those of the metropolitan areas (including Greater London), are given in Table 4. The South East region, containing London, is by far the largest region in terms of population size, totalling nearly 17.8 million, accounting for just over 30 per cent of Britain's population in 1993. The next largest region is the North West, which includes Manchester and Liverpool, with a population of 6.4 million, over 4 million of whom live in the metropolitan areas around these two cities. The smallest region is East Anglia, with a population of 2.1 million. East Anglia is largely rural and has the lowest population density of any of the English regions, 167 people per sq km. The North West and the South East are the most densely populated regions, recording 873 and 653 people per sq km respectively.

About a third of Britain's population lives in the seven English metropolitan areas set out in Table 4. When other non-metropolitan cities and other largely industrial areas are taken into account, well over half of the population lives within a conurbation. London is by far the largest metropolitan area and city with 6.9 million people. The next largest city, Birmingham, is the centre of the West Midlands metropolitan area, and has a population of just over 1 million. Three other cities have populations over half a million. These are Leeds (725,000), Glasgow (681,000) and Sheffield (532,000). Four further cities exceed 400,000 population. These are Manchester, Liverpool, Bradford and Edinburgh.

Table 4: Population Distribution (1993)

	Population (thousands)	Population change 1981–93 %	People per sq km
England	48,533	3.7	372
Wales	2,906	3.3	140
Scotland	5,120	–1.2	66
Northern Ireland	1,632	6.1	120
Britain	**58,191**	**3.3**	**241**
English regions:			
North	3,102	–0.5	201
Yorkshire and Humberside	5,014	1.9	325
East Midlands	4,083	6.0	261
East Anglia	2,094	10.6	167
South East	17,769	4.5	653
South West	4,768	8.8	200
West Midlands	5,290	2.0	407
North West	6,412	–0.7	873
Metropolitan counties:			
Greater London	6,933	1.9	4,393
Greater Manchester	2,579	–1.5	2,006
Merseyside	1,441	–5.3	2,199
South Yorkshire	1,306	–0.8	838
Tyne and Wear	1,138	–1.5	2,106
West Midlands	2,634	–1.5	2,930
West Yorkshire	2,102	1.7	1,033

Sources: OPCS, General Register Office for Scotland and General Register Office for Northern Ireland.

Only about one in ten of Britain's population live in remoter, mainly rural areas. Most of the mountainous parts, including much of Scotland, Wales and Northern Ireland and the Pennines of northern England, are sparsely populated.

Redistribution of Population

While Britain's population increased only slightly, by 3.3 per cent, between 1981 and 1993, there has been a significant redistribution of population within the country. The broad pattern is one of redistribution of population from the north to the south, largely reflecting regional differences in economic fortunes. The four fastest growing English regions are the four most southerly, and the two fastest growing are the most rural: East Anglia experienced an increase in population of over 10 per cent between 1981 and 1993, while the population of the South West grew by almost 9 per cent. The East Midlands and the South East grew by 6 per cent and 4.5 per cent respectively. Northern Ireland also experienced above average growth, with the population rising by 6 per cent to 1.6 million in 1993.

Scotland, the North West (including the metropolitan counties of Greater Manchester and Merseyside) and the North (including Tyne and Wear) all showed a reduction in population during the period (see Table 4). These regions are characterised by population loss from many metropolitan areas, which partly reflects a change in the pattern of employment opportunities as the industrial base of Britain adapted to changing conditions in the 1980s and early 1990s.

A second pattern also emerges within individual regions. There has been a movement from the older inner cities to the suburbs through much of the 19th and 20th centuries. In recent times, there has been a continued reduction in the population of some conurbations—although loss from others has ceased—and a general growth in the population of the surrounding areas. For England and Wales rural areas have generally experienced higher increases in population than urban areas. Although rural areas tend to have an older population and a lower rate of natural change in their population, they have tended to experience substantial net inward migration. Conversely, urban areas have more births than deaths, but they have been affected by net outward migration.

England and Wales

Of the population of England and Wales in mid-1993, just over 18 million (35 per cent) lived in Greater London or other metropolitan counties. Some 33.3 million lived in non-metropolitan areas:

—4.7 million in non-metropolitan cities;

—6.9 million in industrial areas;

—2.4 million in new towns;

—3.7 million in resorts, ports and retirement areas;

—10.1 million in urban and mixed urban/rural areas; and

—5.6 million in remoter, mainly rural areas.

All metropolitan conurbations in England except Greater London and West Yorkshire showed a loss of population between 1981 and 1993. Partly this reflects their changing economic fortunes, with most of them suffering a significant loss of jobs during the 1980s and early 1990s, compared with a general growth in the economies of smaller cities, towns and more accessible rural areas. Partly it also reflects controls on suburban expansion of cities, for example through the use of Green Belt policies, designed partially for the purpose of constraining town and city expansion. This has been possible because of the town and country planning system.[7]

Outside the metropolitan conurbations, the population has generally increased. Between 1981 and 1993 the populations of non-metropolitan cities and industrial areas both rose by about 2 per cent. On the other hand the number of people in remoter rural areas increased by 9 per cent. Around 10 million people live in smaller towns and mixed urban/rural areas, and their numbers increased by 6.5 per cent between 1981 and 1993. In England the county with the largest population growth has been Cambridgeshire, where the population rose by 16 per cent between 1981 and 1993, to 683,000. Six other counties—Buckinghamshire, Cornwall, Dorset, Northamptonshire, Somerset and Wiltshire—experienced growth of over 10 per cent in this period.

About 2.4 million people live in districts containing purpose-built new towns, an increase of 9 per cent between 1981 and 1993. New towns were primarily built to encourage the gradual dispersal of industry and population from congested cities to new areas, which were planned to become self-contained towns with their own industry, services and amenities within convenient distance of the whole community. The fastest growing new town in the 1980s and early 1990s was Milton Keynes (Buckinghamshire), one of the most recent. Its population grew by 46 per cent between 1981 and 1993 to reach 184,000. Other similar districts with high growth (over 15 per cent) between 1981 and 1993 are Bracknell (Berkshire), Northampton, Peterborough (Cambridgeshire) and Redditch (Hereford and Worcester).

Retirement migration to coastal resorts and a limited number of inland retirement areas remains popular, but these areas also

[7] For information on the planning system see *Planning* (Aspects of Britain: HMSO, 1992).

offer attractive environments for people to live and work. These types of location also experienced a population increase of 9 per cent between 1981 and 1993. Much of the growth in the South West can be associated with this type of effect. In the three coastal counties of Cornwall, Devon and Dorset over half of the local authority districts recorded population increases of more than 10 per cent between 1981 and 1993.

In Wales just over 60 per cent of the population live in the southern counties of Mid, South and West Glamorgan and Gwent. Population growth has recently occurred mainly in rural areas, with the population of Powys rising by 8 per cent between 1981 and 1993. The rate of growth also exceeded 5 per cent in Clwyd, Dyfed and South Glamorgan. The city of Cardiff experienced a rise of 6 per cent, with the population reaching 298,700 in 1993. However, several areas have experienced falls in population, including a number where the traditional industries of coalmining or steelmaking were important, such as Port Talbot, Rhondda and Blaenau Gwent.

Scotland

There have been wide variations in the rate of change of population in Scotland. Although the population of Scotland in 1993 was about 60,000 (1.2 per cent) lower than in 1981, two regions—Grampian and Highland—recorded population growth above the average for Britain. Between 1981 and 1993 their populations rose by 8.9 and 6.2 per cent respectively. In Grampian the districts of Kincardine and Deeside, and Gordon had particularly high increases, of 32 and 25 per cent respectively. The largest population fall, of 13 per cent, was recorded in Shetland, mainly reflecting the loss of oil terminal construction workers temporarily resident in

1981, while the population of the Western Isles fell by 7 per cent. The region of Strathclyde experienced a fall of 5 per cent in population, while some parts of the region, such as the City of Glasgow, Clydebank and Inverclyde districts, recorded falls of over 10 per cent.

Northern Ireland

In Northern Ireland population grew in all but two of the 26 districts—Belfast and Strabane—between 1981 and 1993. The population of Belfast, where 18 per cent of the population live, fell by 6 per cent to 296,700 in 1993. Eight districts—Ards, Banbridge, Carrickfergus, Coleraine, Down, Limavady, Lisburn and Magherafelt—recorded an increase of over 10 per cent. The largest rise was in Lisburn, where the population grew by 23 per cent to 104,100.

Natural Change

Much of the redistribution of population occurs through population movement from one area to another (see p. 33). However, the process of 'natural change', through births and deaths, can also lead to the population of some areas growing in numbers and others declining. Where areas have a large proportion of young adults, their populations are likely to have more births and fewer deaths, and hence the population grows. Just over half of the population growth in England and Wales due to natural change occurred in the South East region between 1981 and 1991, while the South West lost population through natural change, as deaths outnumbered births. Within England and Wales, over a quarter of all counties experienced such a natural loss of population. Virtually all were coastal counties with a high proportion of the elderly. The most extreme case is the county of East Sussex, which lost 5 per cent of its population between 1981 and 1991 in this way, although this loss was more than offset by net inward migration. By contrast, three counties in the South East gained more than 5 per cent through natural growth: Buckinghamshire, Berkshire and Bedfordshire. Among the metropolitan areas, Greater London and the West Midlands also experienced higher than average rates of natural growth, exceeding 3 per cent over the period, with births greatly exceeding deaths, by 242,000 and 86,000 respectively.

Natural changes though may be outweighed by the effects of migration into or out of the area. For example, all 15 counties in England and Wales with natural declines in their population between 1981 and 1991 experienced overall population growth as a result of migration.

Migration

There are two important types of migration. First, there is the pattern of movement into and out of the country, known as international migration. This influences the size of the national population as well as the ethnic mix. Secondly, there is the pattern of movement within the country, affecting the distribution of population between and within regions. This is known as internal migration.

Migration can be considered in terms of 'gross' flows, the movements out of an area and the movements into an area, or 'net' flows, the difference between the gross flows. Measurement of levels of gross or net migration are less precise than for other demographic processes because there is no complete registration process.

The definition used by Britain of an international migrant is the standard definition adopted by the United Nations. A migrant into Britain is somebody who, having lived elsewhere for at least 12 months, declares an intention on entering Britain of residing in Britain for at least 12 months. Anyone doing the reverse is a migrant out of Britain. The International Passenger Survey provides estimates of these movements, but does not include movements between Britain and the Irish Republic or movements of the armed forces and their dependants. However, OPCS produces figures taking account of these and other changes, such as asylum seekers. Statistics on this basis are given in Table 5.

International Migration

For much of Britain's history, more migrants left Britain than entered. In the early decades of the 20th century, the net loss exceeded 50,000 people a year (see Table 2). As late as the 1970s, that continued to be the case. In the five-year period 1978–82, according to the International Passenger Survey, on average 220,400 people left the country a year and 182,100 entered, giving a net annual loss of 38,300 people a year (see Table 6). This pattern was generally reversed in the 1980s, mainly reflecting a higher inflow than before.

In 1990 and 1991 some 267,000 people entered Britain, according to the International Passenger Survey. However, in 1992 there was a decline in both the numbers entering and leaving the country, to 216,000 and 227,000 respectively, resulting in an overall net loss of 11,000, after three successive years of net gain. However, on the basis of OPCS estimates—which take account of movements to and from the Irish Republic, people seeking asylum after entering the country and other people admitted as short-term visitors who are subsequently allowed to stay for a year or longer— there was net civilian inward migration of about 34,000. This still represented a substantially lower net inflow than in the three previous years.

Table 5: International Civilian Migration 1986–92

Thousands

	1986	1987	1988	1989	1990	1991	1992
International Passenger Survey Statistics:							
Inflow	250	212	216	250	267	267	216
Outflow	213	210	237	205	231	239	227
Balance	37	2	–21	44	36	28	–11
Others:							
Asylum seekers and other visitor 'switchers'	14	14	17	28	44	48	49
Net inflow to/from Irish Republic	7	14	22	19	8	–2	–4
Total net inflow	**58**	**30**	**18**	**91**	**88**	**74**	**34**

Source: OPCS.

Note: Differences between totals and the sums of their component parts are due to rounding.

Young adults form an above average proportion of international migrants to and from Britain. About 30 per cent of international migrants were aged between 16 and 24 in 1992, as against 15 per cent of the population. A lower than average proportion of migrants were elderly people.

Australia is currently the single most important country in terms of population exchange with Britain, accounting for 11 per cent of people entering Britain and 17 per cent of those leaving Britain in the five-year period 1988–92. Including Australia, the

Table 6: Net International Migration by Country[a]
Thousands (annual average)

	1978–82	1983–87	1988–92
Commonwealth countries[b]	–6.4	16.1	13.0
of which:			
Australia	*–21.9*	*–12.0*	*–12.0*
Canada	*–13.1*	*–1.4*	*–4.0*
New Zealand	*–3.0*	*1.3*	*5.7*
African Commonwealth	*3.1*	*6.8*	*6.3*
Bangladesh, India,			
Sri Lanka	*13.6*	*10.5*	*8.4*
Pakistan	*11.4*	*8.5*	*6.5*
Caribbean	*0.9*	*0.8*	*0.4*
Other	*2.7*	*1.7*	*1.6*
European Union	–3.0	7.3	4.2
United States	–10.6	–5.0	–9.0
Total non-Commonwealth	–31.9	14.3	2.1
All countries	–38.3	30.4	15.1
British citizens	*–75.6*	*–15.3*	*–31.0*
Non-British citizens	*37.3*	*45.7*	*46.1*

Source: OPCS.

[a] Excludes movements between Britain and the Irish Republic.
[b] Excludes South Africa.
Note: A positive figure indicates that inflow from this area exceeds the outflow to that area.

Commonwealth countries[8] accounted for 40 per cent of all movements. A further 10 per cent of those entering Britain in this period came from the United States, which received 15 per cent of

[8] Excluding South Africa, which rejoined the Commonwealth in 1994.

people leaving Britain. In 1992 the United States was the largest single destination for migrants from Britain, receiving some 37,000 people. Over the period 1988 to 1992 about 26 per cent of all movements were between Britain and the other countries of the European Union, and a further 6 per cent of moves were with other European countries. Together, the Commonwealth, the EU and the United States account for over three-quarters of all of Britain's international migration.

Much of the growth in Britain's international migration over the last 15 years has resulted from the increasing importance of movements between Britain and the rest of the European Union, which have doubled in number since the late 1970s.

About 400,000 British nationals live in other EU countries. The largest concentrations are in Germany (103,000), the Irish Republic (58,000) and France and Spain (each with 50,000). Some 772,000 other EU nationals live in Britain, of whom about 510,000 (66 per cent) are nationals of the Irish Republic. Excluding the Irish Republic, more British nationals live in the rest of the EU than vice versa. After the Irish Republic, Italy has the most nationals living in Britain, with 86,000 in 1991.

International migration to and from Britain is a mixture of British citizens and non-British citizens. Just over half of all these international movements involved British citizens in the 1988-92 period, according to the International Passenger Survey statistics. In terms of net movement, however, there was a net loss of British citizens, averaging 31,000 a year and a net gain of 46,000 non-British citizens during the same period. The most important combined net losses during the 1988–92 period were to Australia, the United States and Canada (12,000, 9,000 and 4,000 a year respectively, see Table 6). The most significant net gains were from the

South Asian sub-continent, the African countries of the Commonwealth and New Zealand. In part this reflects international labour mobility and the pattern of job opportunities around the world.

In 1993 some 55,600 people were accepted for settlement under the Immigration Rules, of whom 25 per cent were from the South Asian sub-continent, 20 per cent from the rest of Asia, 19 per cent from Africa and 14 per cent from the Americas. Wives and husbands of British subjects already here were respectively 19,100 and 12,000, representing in total over half of acceptances.

As elsewhere in Europe, Britain has experienced in recent years a large increase in the number of people seeking asylum, although the number of applications fell substantially in 1992 and 1993 following the introduction of new administrative procedures aimed at curbing multiple applications and other abuses of the system. In 1993 asylum applications totalled 22,400. Of these, 1,600 people were recognised as refugees and granted asylum, and 11,100 were not recognised as refugees but were granted exceptional leave to stay in Britain.

Internal Migration

The Census of Population provides information on the patterns of migration. About 10 per cent of the residents of Great Britain aged one and over at the time of the Census in 1991 were at a different address compared with a year earlier. Above average rates of movement were recorded in parts of London, a number of districts in a ring around 100 to 150 km to the north and west of London, and parts of northern and western Scotland. Relatively low rates of movement were evident in south Wales, the West Midlands and Merseyside. Over half of all moves within Great Britain were to an address within 5 km of the original address, and two-thirds were less than 10 km away. Only one in seven of people moving had moved more than 80 km. Internal migration rates were highest for unemployed people and lowest for self-employed men and part-time women employees.

Registration of people with NHS doctors, as recorded by the National Health Service Central Registers (NHSCR), is another measure for assessing internal migration. In 1992 there were 1.8 million population moves between Family Health Services Areas in Britain. These broadly correspond to shire counties and metropolitan districts. About half of these (over 900,000) represented inter-regional movements, which correspond to longer distance moves.

Recent trends in internal migration derived from NHSCR re-registrations are given in Table 7. Two main trends have taken place: a general pattern of movement from the northern and peripheral regions to the more buoyant economy of southern England and a move away from the older inner city areas.

The national figures have tended to show a loss of population by internal migration for Scotland and Northern Ireland, while England and Wales have experienced an increase in population through net migration. However, since 1989 England has had a net loss of population through internal migration, while Scotland has had a net gain. Movements in 1993 between the constituent countries of Britain showed a net loss of 9,700 in England and a small net loss in Northern Ireland, while Scotland and Wales had net increases.

Looking at the English regions, the North West and the West Midlands have tended to experience a net loss of population through internal migration, although the largest regional loss has been in the South East. This though almost wholly reflects the

Table 7: Net Migration within Britain

Thousands

	1981	1986	1991	1992	1993
England	1.5	14.9	−16.4	−11.4	−9.7
Wales	2.7	5.4	4.0	3.5	3.2
Scotland	−1.3	−14.1	9.2	7.2	7.2
Northern Ireland	−2.9	-6.3	3.2	0.7	-0.8
English regions:					
North	−7.9	−7.1	0.3	0.9	−3.2
Yorkshire and Humberside	−5.1	−11.9	−0.4	1.9	0.3
East Midlands	4.8	17.1	8.1	9.6	10.1
East Anglia	10.8	10.3	10.4	8.0	8.5
South East	9.7	−4.2	−41.7	−36.7	−27.8
of which Greater London	*−32.0*	*−49.6*	*−53.3*	*−51.6*	*−52.9*
South West	20.2	46.4	21.8	21.0	20.5
West Midlands	−11.6	−7.8	−5.2	−6.5	−9.2
North West	−19.5	−27.9	−9.8	−9.6	−8.8

Sources: OPCS, General Register Office for Scotland and General Register Office for Northern Ireland.

migration of people out of Greater London. For example, in 1993 while Greater London lost 52,900 people through net internal migration, the rest of the South East had a net gain of 25,000. The South West, East Anglia and the East Midlands have consistently experienced net gains through internal migration, the largest being for the South West.

The move away from large urban and industrial areas to the smaller towns and rural areas has continued. For example, Greater London has lost population through net outward migration. It has done so despite large net gains through international migration. The net outward migration with the rest of Britain averaged over 50,000 people a year in the last seven years.

The other large conurbations have also experienced falls in population. Between them the metropolitan cities lost 40,000 people a year through net outward migration between 1981 and 1991.

Planned urban growth, in the form of new towns (see p. 25), resulted in a modest net inward migration of 8,000 people a year between 1981 and 1991. The bulk of the movement from the conurbations was to three categories of area. Some 42,000 people a year (net) migrated into resorts, port and retirement areas. A high proportion were already retired or were in late middle age and moving work location in anticipation of retirement. About 23,000 a year (net) migrated into smaller town locations (urban and mixed urban/rural), while 44,000 a year (net) migrated into remoter, mainly rural areas. Rural areas and small towns in the South West and East Anglia have absorbed much of this migration, especially from the South East.

Ethnic Minorities

Britain has a long history of accommodating minority groups and in the last 100 years or so a variety of people have settled in the country, some to avoid political or religious persecution and others seeking a better way of life or an escape from poverty.

The Irish have long made homes in Britain and formed a significant section of the population; some 837,000 residents in Great Britain recorded in the 1991 Census were born in Northern Ireland or the Irish Republic. Many Jewish refugees started a new life in Britain towards the end of the 19th century and in the 1930s, and after 1945 large numbers of other European refugees, particularly Poles, settled in Britain. Substantial immigration from the Caribbean and the South Asian sub-continent dates mainly from the 1950s and the 1960s. In recent years the number of people coming from the South Asian sub-continent has remained roughly stable, but there has been a rise in immigration from some African countries, such as Ghana and Nigeria.

According to the question on ethnic grouping in the 1991 Census of Population, 94.5 per cent of the population in Great Britain belonged to the 'white' group, while just over 3 million people described themselves as belonging to another ethnic group, 5.5 per cent of the population. The largest individual ethnic minority group was Indian, with some 840,000 people (1.5 per cent of the population and 28 per cent of the ethnic minority population as a whole). However, the three black categories together (Caribbean, African and 'Other') constitute a slightly higher proportion—1.6 per cent of the population. Pakistanis form 0.9 per cent of the population, with Bangladeshis and Chinese each accounting for 0.3 per cent.

Over half of all those belonging to ethnic minority groups have migrated to Britain as international migrants. The remaining 47 per cent were born in Britain, although this proportion varies from group to group (see Table 8). For instance, only around a quarter of the Chinese group were born in Britain compared with over half of all black Caribbeans. Even when born outside Britain, ethnic minority groups have not necessarily arrived in Britain directly from their country of ethnic origin. For instance, over a quarter of the overseas-born Indian group were born in East Africa and two-thirds of the overseas-born Chinese group were born in Hong Kong, Malaysia or Singapore.

Another important characteristic of ethnic minorities is their relatively young age structure. About a third of the people belonging to ethnic minorities are under the age of 16, compared with 20 per cent for the population of Great Britain as a whole (see Table 8). Only 3 per cent of ethnic minority groups are over the age of 65, compared with 16 per cent for Great Britain's population as a whole.

In 1991 the total period fertility rate (TPFR, see p. 53) for mothers born in the New Commonwealth (all Commonwealth countries except Australia, Canada and New Zealand) was significantly higher, at 2.5 children per woman, than that for British-born mothers, who averaged 1.8. In 1991, 7 per cent of all live births in England and Wales were to women born in the New Commonwealth. For Pakistanis and Bangladeshis the equivalent TPFR was much higher, at 4.6. This rate had, however, fallen very significantly over time, from 8.8 in 1971.

Distribution

Britain's ethnic minority population is heavily concentrated in industrial and urban areas, with over two-thirds living in four

Table 8: Ethnic Groups in Great Britain 1991

	Number (*thousands*)	% born in Britain	Age distribution (%) 0–4	5–15	65 and over
White	51,874	96	6	13	17
Black:					
Caribbean	500	54	8	14	6
African	212	36	12	18	1
Other	178	85	20	30	1
Indian	840	42	9	21	4
Pakistani	477	51	13	30	2
Bangladeshi	163	37	15	32	1
Chinese	157	29	7	16	3
Other groups	488	44	13	22	3
All minority groups	3,015	47	11	22	3
All groups	54,889	93	7	13	16

Sources: OPCS and General Register Office for Scotland.

conurbations: London, the West Midlands, West Yorkshire and Greater Manchester. Over half of the ethnic minority population live in the South East, compared with 31 per cent of the population as a whole, with Greater London containing nearly 45 per cent of people from ethnic minority groups (as against 10 per cent of people from the white ethnic group). Around 10 per cent of the population of the South East belongs to an ethnic minority group (20 per cent for Greater London). The English regions with the lowest proportions are the North (1.3 per cent) and the South West (1.4 per cent). In many rural districts of these regions less than 1 per cent of the population are from ethnic minority groups.

Ethnic minority groups in Scotland and Wales also account for just over 1 per cent of the population. In Scotland ethnic minorities number about 63,000 and their greatest concentration is in Strathclyde, especially the city of Glasgow. In the 1991 Census in Northern Ireland people were asked to state their country of birth, but not their ethnic group. Those born in Asian countries numbered nearly 3,700.

The local authority district with the highest proportion of ethnic minority groups is the London borough of Brent (45 per cent in 1991), while ethnic minority groups account for more than 30 per cent of the population in five other London boroughs: Newham, Tower Hamlets, Hackney, Ealing and Lambeth. Outside London the main concentrations of ethnic minorities are in Leicester (where ethnic minority groups accounted for 28.5 per cent of the population in 1991), Slough, Bradford, the West Midlands and the Pennine conurbations.

Regional concentrations vary considerably among ethnic groups. For example, about 60 per cent of people from black ethnic groups live in London, compared with about 40 per cent of Indians and 18 per cent of Pakistanis. Pakistanis though were concentrated more in other metropolitan areas, such as the West Midlands and West Yorkshire. The black Caribbean ethnic group has high concentrations in inner and south London and Birmingham, with smaller local concentrations in Greater Manchester, West Yorkshire and South Yorkshire. Over three-quarters of black Africans live in Greater London, especially in inner and north-west London. Outside London there are smaller concentrations in the port cities of Cardiff and Liverpool and in the university cities of

Oxford and Cambridge. The 'black other' group is more dispersed, although with local concentrations in most areas of ethnic minority group settlement.

Over 40 per cent of the Indian ethnic group live in Greater London, especially in west and east London, with over 10 per cent of the population in six London boroughs—Brent, Ealing, Harrow, Hounslow, Newham and Redbridge—being in the Indian group. The concentration in west London extends westwards into Berkshire, including Slough. Outside the South East the largest concentration is in Leicester (where 22 per cent of the city's population is Indian). Other concentrations are in Birmingham, Wolverhampton, some other parts of the West and East Midlands, Blackburn, Greater Manchester and West Yorkshire.

The Pakistani ethnic group has by far the lowest proportion of any significant ethnic minority group living in Greater London, while the proportion living in the South East—30 per cent—is similar to that for the white ethnic group. There is a notable concentration of the Pakistani group in the area of the 'mill towns' through south Lancashire into Greater Manchester and West Yorkshire. Nearly 10 per cent of the population of Bradford and over 9 per cent of that of Pendle are Pakistani, while other districts in this area with a relatively high proportion include Blackburn, Rochdale and Hyndburn. Other areas with a relatively high concentration—over 5 per cent of the population—include Slough, Birmingham, the London boroughs of Waltham Forest and Newham, and Luton, while other local concentrations occur in Stafford, Peterborough, Middlesbrough, Newcastle upon Tyne, Lanarkshire, Newport (Gwent) and Cardiff.

By far the largest local concentration of the Bangladeshi ethnic group is in the London borough of Tower Hamlets, where

Bangladeshis accounted for over 22 per cent of the population in 1991. The next highest concentration was in the neighbouring borough of Newham, where Bangladeshis formed just under 4 per cent of the inhabitants. Other local concentrations occur in some other inner London boroughs (including Camden and Westminster), Luton and Oldham, with smaller groups in other areas such as the West Midlands metropolitan county and some other Pennine mill towns.

The Chinese are the least likely of the main ethnic minority groups to live in metropolitan areas and the distribution is much more dispersed than for other minority groups. Their largest shares of the population are in inner London, Merseyside and Greater Manchester. Outside London over half of the Chinese live in non-metropolitan areas.

Language

English is the language predominantly spoken by people in Britain. It is also one of the most widely used in the world. Recent estimates suggest that 310 million people speak it as their first language, with a similar number speaking it as a second language.

Other languages are also spoken in Britain. In Wales, Welsh, a form of Celtic language, was spoken by 19 per cent of the population aged three and over in 1991: some 508,000 people. The distribution of the language is uneven however, and in much of rural north and west Wales Welsh remains the first language of most of the population. Over 60 per cent of people in the districts of Arfon, Dinefwr, Dwyfor, Meirionydd and Ynys Môn—Isle of Anglesey— were Welsh speakers. By contrast, in the southern counties of South Glamorgan and Gwent only 6.5 per cent and 2.4 per cent of the population respectively spoke Welsh. There is some evidence that the decline in the number of Welsh speakers is now being halted, with increasing numbers of children and young people able to speak Welsh and a revival of the language in the largely anglicised areas of south-east and north-east Wales. In 1991 just over a quarter of families with at least one child aged 3 to 15 had one or more children who spoke Welsh.[9]

In Scotland, in 1991 about 70,000 people (1.5 per cent of the population) had some knowledge of Gaelic in that they could speak, read or write the language. Gaelic speakers—totalling 66,000 people (1.4 per cent)—were heavily concentrated in the western Highlands and Islands. Some 68 per cent of residents aged three and over in the Western Isles were Gaelic speakers, and 42 per cent in Skye and Lochalsh. In some other areas in the north-west, there were also significant numbers of Gaelic speakers, but elsewhere in Scotland very few people spoke the language.

A few families in Northern Ireland still speak the Irish form of Gaelic. In the 1991 Census about 142,000 people aged three or over were recorded as having some knowledge of the language in that they could read, speak or write it.

[9] For more information on the Welsh language see *Wales* (Aspects of Britain: HMSO, 1993).

Age Structure

There have been some significant changes in the age structure of the population during the 20th century. Improvements in life expectancy have resulted in a large increase in the numbers of adults surviving into old age. There has thus been a growth in the proportion over pensionable age (60 for women and 65 for men), while the proportion of young people has been declining.

Lower birth rates are reflected in the decline in the proportion of the population who are aged under 16. This has fallen from 25.5 per cent in 1971 to 20.6 per cent in 1993 and after a rise to 20.7 per cent in 2001 the fall is projected to resume, reaching 18.3 per cent in 2021 and 17.6 per cent in 2041. On the other hand there has been an increase in the proportion over 65, with a doubling in the last 30 years of those over 80.

Sex Structure

In mid-1993 the population comprised 29.7 million females and 28.5 million males, representing a ratio of about 104 females to every 100 males. On average though there are about 4 per cent more male births than female births every year. Consequently, in childhood and young adulthood males outnumber females. However, women tend to live longer than men. With the higher mortality of men at all ages, there is a turning point, at about 50 years of age, beyond which the number of women exceeds the number of men. Beyond the age of 60 women significantly outnumber men. By about the age of 80 there are more than twice as many women as men.

Table 9: Age Structure				*% in each age group*	
	Under 16	16–39	40–64	65–79	80 and over
1961	24.9	31.4	32.0	9.8	1.9
1971	25.5	31.3	29.9	10.9	2.3
1981	22.3	34.9	27.8	12.2	2.8
1991	20.3	35.3	28.6	12.0	3.7
1993	20.6	34.9	28.8	11.9	3.9
Mid-year projections					
2001	20.7	32.9	30.6	11.4	4.3
2011	19.2	30.0	34.1	11.9	4.7
2021	18.3	29.7	32.7	14.3	5.1
2031	18.2	28.4	30.5	16.3	6.6
2041	17.6	27.8	30.1	16.8	7.8
2051	17.6	28.0	30.3	14.9	9.2

Sources: OPCS, Government Actuary's Department, General Register Offices for Scotland and Northern Ireland.

Children

The gradual fall in the birth rate from the relatively high levels of the 19th and early 20th centuries is reflected in the decline in the number of children. There were fewer children in 1991 than in 1901. While 32 per cent of Britain's population was under the age of 15 in 1901, this proportion had dropped to 19 per cent by 1993.

The pattern has not been one of continual decline. 'Baby booms' have occurred, for example during the years 1947 to 1951, following the Second World War, and also during the 1960s (see p. 50). There was, however, a decline in the number of children from 1972 until 1988. Since then there has been a small increase, which is reflected in the forecast rise in the proportion of children by 2001 (see p. 45).

In 1981 there were 12.5 million people aged under 16 in Britain, amounting to 22.3 per cent of the total population. In 1993 the number was 12 million, 20.6 per cent of the total population. Among the school-age population (those aged 5 to 15 inclusive), numbers fell by 11 per cent, from 9.1 to 8.1 million between 1981 and 1993. This substantial reduction has had a significant impact on the provision of education services during the period.[10] However, as birth rates have increased (see p. 50), so the number of those aged under five has increased by 13 per cent, from 3.5 million in 1981 to 3.9 million in 1993.

Northern Ireland has the highest proportion of young people in Britain. Over one-quarter of its population in 1993 was aged under 16: 8 per cent under five and 17.7 per cent aged 5 to 15. Some of the lowest proportions of young people are found in areas with a high proportion of elderly and retired people, such as the southern coastal counties. Dorset had the lowest proportion of under 16s in 1992, 17.7 per cent: 5.6 per cent under five and 12.1 per cent in the 5–15 age group. However, the Isle of Wight recorded the lowest proportion of young children: 5.5 per cent of the population was under five.

Working-age Population

The number of people of working age (men aged 16–64 and women 16–59) has increased considerably during the 20th century,

---

[10] For information on the changing provision of education services see *Education* (Aspects of Britain: HMSO, 1995).

although the proportion of the total population in 1993—61 per cent—is similar to that at the same ages at the beginning of the century. In 1993 there were 35.6 million people of working age in Britain, having risen from 32.5 million in 1971. During the period 1981 to 1993 the number of people of working age increased by 1.8 million, 5 per cent. The largest increase (of 16 per cent) was experienced in the 25–44 age group. The number of people in older working-age groups—45 to 64 (for men) or 59 (for women)—remained fairly stable, at around 10.8 million during the 1980s, but increased by 5 per cent between 1991 and 1993 to 11.4 million.

However, the decline in the number of children during the last two decades will have an eventual impact on the labour market. Although the working-age population is predicted to rise into the early 21st century, it is then projected to decline to 34.6 million by 2031.

Elderly People

One of the most significant changes in Britain's age structure in the 20th century is the growth in the numbers of elderly people. In 1901 there were just 2.4 million people over retirement age (60 for women, 65 for men). By 1993 there were 10.6 million, accounting for 18.3 per cent of the population, compared with 6.2 per cent in 1901. Nearly two-thirds of the population over retirement age are female.

Between 1981 and 1993 the number of people over retirement age grew by 6 per cent. This increase was heavily concentrated in the very elderly. There was a 63 per cent increase in the number of people aged over 85 to 982,000, and a 13 per cent increase in those aged between 75 and 84 to 3 million, although there has been a slight decline in numbers in the latter group since 1990. The number of younger pensioners aged 65 to 74 (for men) and 60 to 74 (for women), 6.6 million in 1993, was slightly lower than the number in 1981. The number of people who reach 100, although still very small, is much higher than before. For example, in England and Wales there were 4,390 people aged 100 and over in 1991, compared with just an estimated 300 in 1951. The growth in the very elderly is expected to continue. The number of people aged 75 and over in Britain is projected to grow from 4 million in mid-1993 to 4.5 million in 2003, representing an increase of 13 per cent.

There are quite wide variations in the distribution of the elderly. Coastal resorts, such as Scarborough and Blackpool, are one of the main types of area having relatively large proportions of the elderly. Southern coastal counties tend to have some of the highest proportions of people over pensionable age. The Isle of Wight had the highest level by county of people over pensionable age in 1993—26.5 per cent—while the districts of Christchurch in Dorset and Rother in East Sussex had over one-third of their populations over pensionable age. Among the very elderly—those of 75 and over—Rother had the highest rate in 1992 (15.7 per cent), while Worthing, Christchurch, Eastbourne and Arun (West Sussex) each had over 14 per cent aged 75 or more. On the other hand new towns, such as Milton Keynes, have some of the lowest proportions of elderly people. Northern Ireland also has a relatively low proportion of pensioners.

The growth in the proportion of the population above retirement age has resulted in an increase in the ratio of those of pensionable age to those of working age, from around 21 per cent in 1951 to 30 per cent in 1993. It is projected to increase further, reaching 46 per cent by 2031. Another ratio considered important when considering the ability of the working population to support dependants is the dependency ratio, which represents the combined number of children and pensioners for every 100 people of working age. This has risen from 57 in 1951 to 64 in 1993, but is forecast to rise more rapidly in the 21st century, reaching 82 by 2036.

Continued increases in the size of the elderly population have an important implication for social welfare provision—particularly pensions, caring services and health services. The rapid growth in the 'very elderly' is expected to have a particularly significant impact on the latter two services and to increase pressures on institutional health and residential care services. New policies on community care in England, Scotland and Wales have been implemented under the NHS and Community Care Act 1990. Similar arrangements for Northern Ireland were introduced in 1993 under equivalent legislation. The new arrangements are aimed at providing a network of support for those requiring welfare and health care, but who are also in a position to remain in their own home.[11] Local authorities increasingly act as enablers and commissioners of services after assessing the needs of their populations for social care. Between 1978–79 and 1992–93 spending on health care for elderly people increased by over 40 per cent and net spending on social services by 68 per cent in real terms. Services for elderly people are designed to help them live at home whenever possible. However, about 5 per cent of those aged 65 or over currently live in residential homes.

[11] For further information see *Social Welfare* (Aspects of Britain: HMSO, 1995).

Births

In 1993 there were 762,000 births in Britain, the lowest figure since 1986, but still slightly higher than the annual average for the 1980s of 750,000. Contributory factors to the relatively low level of births in recent years include:

—the trends towards later marriage and towards postponing births;

—the current preference for smaller families than in the past, reflected in a significant decline in the proportion of families with four or more children; and

—more widespread and effective contraception, making it easier to plan families.

Projected levels of births are expected to decline to around 700,000–720,000 a year in the next century, and to fall to below 700,000 a year by the 2040s (see Table 2).

Birth Rates

Changes in the rate of child-bearing are shown for selected years in Table 10. The 1960s 'baby boom' reached its peak in 1964 when there were over 1 million live births. By contrast 1977 represents the lowest point in the subsequent trough, with births falling to 657,000. Births then rose and, as the generation born in the 1960s baby boom reached its most fertile time of life, there was a 'mini-boom' in live births in the late 1980s. This reached its peak around 1990 when there were 799,000 live births, and births have been falling since then.

These fluctuations in the number of births are also reflected in the changes in the various rates used to measure the rate of child-bearing. The crude birth rate measures the annual number of births per 1,000 people. At its peak in 1964 this reached a level of 18.8, but by 1977 it had declined significantly to its low point of 11.7. The crude birth rate then generally rose, reaching 13.9 in 1990, but falling since then to 13.1 in 1993. Birth rates vary within Britain. The highest rate is in Northern Ireland, 15.3 live births per 1,000 people in 1993. Southern coastal counties of England tend to have relatively low birth rates, and the lowest rate recorded in 1992, 10.5, was in the Isle of Wight.

Table 10: Birth Statistics

	1964	1977	1986	1991	1992	1993
Live births ('000s)	1,015	657	755	793	781	762
Crude birth rate[a]	18.8	11.7	13.3	13.7	13.5	13.1
General fertility rate[b]	94	59	61	64	63	62
Total period fertility rate[c]	2.95	1.69	1.78	1.83	1.81	1.76
Mean age at maternity (England and Wales)	27.2	26.5	27.0	27.7	27.9	28.1
Live births outside marriage ('000s)	70.0	62.7	158.5	236.1	240.8	241.8
% of live births outside marriage	7	10	21	30	31	32

Sources: OPCS and General Register Offices for Scotland and Northern Ireland.
[a] Number per 1,000 population.
[b] Number in relation to number of women aged 15 to 44.
[c] Average number of children who would be born per woman if women experienced the age-specific fertility rates of the period in question throughout their child-bearing life span.

Fertility Rates

The general fertility rate defines the rate in terms of the annual number of births per 1,000 women of child-bearing age (generally taken as 15–44). Changes in the general fertility rate mirror those of the 35 per cent reduction in the number of births between 1964 and 1977, falling from 94 to 59 over that period, a fall of 37 per cent. Since the low point of 1977, there has been a modest rise, reaching 64 by 1990, but declining slightly since then to 62 (see Table 10).

Within the age range of 15–44 there are different child-bearing tendencies at different ages. The most likely age group at which to bear a child is 25–29, at a rate in England and Wales of 117 births per 1,000 women aged 25–29 in 1992, followed by the age groups of 30–34 and 20–24, with rates of 87 and 86 births respectively.

The reduction in fertility rates from 1964 to the trough of 1977 was substantial across all age groups, with the greatest proportional reductions occurring among older age groups. This was reflected in a reduction in the average (mean) age of the mother at childbirth from 27.3 in 1964 to 26.5 in 1977. This represented a continuation of the post-war trend; in 1951, for example, the average age at maternity was 28.4 years old. However, more recently the average age has risen (see p. 53). Fertility rates in all age groups have shown an increase, except in recent years for the 20–24 and 25–29 age groups, where they have declined in England and Wales by 18 and 9 per cent respectively between 1981 and 1992. Fertility rates among women in their thirties rose considerably in this period, by 54 per cent for those aged 35 to 39 and by 27 per cent for those between 30 and 34. Teenage fertility rates also rose, though to a lesser degree, by 17 per cent between 1981 and 1991, but there has subsequently been a fall.

The reduction in the proportion of women in their twenties bearing children between 1964 and 1991 is the major demographic cause of the overall reduction in the numbers of births over this period. This reduction is also reflected in the 'total period fertility rate' (TPFR), which is defined as the average number of children who would be born per woman if women experienced the age-specific fertility rates of the period in question throughout their child-bearing life span. Although this is only a notional measure of completed family size, it is the one generally considered most accurately to depict the overall child-bearing rate in any given year. In the peak of the 'baby boom' in 1964, the TPFR was 2.95 (children per woman). By 1977 it had fallen to 1.69, but it then rose again by the early 1980s. During the 1980s there was relatively little change. Since 1990 there has been a slight decline in the TPFR to 1.76 in 1993 (see Table 10).

There is a significant variation in the TPFR within Britain. In 1992 Northern Ireland had the highest value (2.1) and Scotland the lowest (1.67). However, the TPFR for Northern Ireland was over 17 per cent lower than in 1982. In England the regional values ranged from 1.88 in the West Midlands to 1.75 in Greater London. In Wales the TPFR was 1.87.

Current projections of births (see Table 2) assume that the TPFR will increase to 1.88 and will remain at that level thereafter. In order for Britain's population to replace itself naturally in the long term the TPFR needs to be at least 2.1. At rates below this level, deaths will eventually outnumber births and the population will slowly fall in number, as is eventually projected during the 21st century (see p. 12).

Women are tending to give birth to children at a later age. The mean age at birth for mothers in England and Wales rose from 26.2 years in 1971 to 27.9 in 1992 and 28.1 in 1993. Within marriage the most noticeable trend is the deferment of the birth of the first child, from 24.7 years in 1961 to 27.8 in 1992, the highest ever recorded. However, the average age of a mother at the birth of the fourth child has varied little over the last three decades, being the same in 1992 as it was in 1961, at 31.6 years. Intervals between the average age at first and subsequent births have shortened considerably from 2.7 to 1.4 years between first and second births and from 2.4 to 1.3 years between second and third births, over the period from 1961 to 1992.

Births outside Marriage

Of the 762,000 births in 1993, only 520,000 were recorded within marriage, the lowest number this century. By contrast, births out-side marriage have steadily increased to record levels, reaching 241,800 in 1993, 32 per cent of all births. This compares with only 8 per cent of live births being outside marriage in 1966 and 12.5 per cent in 1981.

The substantial rise in births outside marriage has occurred in all parts of Britain. Within Britain the highest levels of births out-side marriage are in the North West and North regions (37 and 36 per cent respectively in 1992). The metropolitan counties of Merseyside and Cleveland experienced the highest rates: 42 per cent. East Anglia has the lowest level of the English regions—26 per cent—but the lowest rate is in Northern Ireland (22 per cent). By county the lowest rate in Great Britain is in Surrey (just under 20 per cent).

Although the number of births outside marriage has increased in all age groups, they are most prevalent in teenage mothers and those under 25. The majority of births in England and Wales to women under 25 are outside marriage: 84 per cent for women under 20 and 47 per cent for women aged 20–24. For births outside marriage the average age of motherhood is considerably less than for those within marriage, standing in England and Wales at 25.2 years in 1992, having risen from 23.5 years in 1981. In 1992, 19 per cent of such births were to women under the age of 20, compared with under 2 per cent for married women of the same age. About 46 per cent of births outside marriage were to women aged 25 or over.

The growth in the numbers of births to young mothers outside marriage is associated with the growth in the number of lone parent families (otherwise known as single parents) and cohabitation, which are considered on pp. 70 and 79.

Family Planning

One of the most significant reasons for the continuing low child-bearing rate across the industrialised world in the late 20th century is the growth in the control of conception and pregnancy through the use of family planning measures.

In Great Britain in 1991 there were over 12 million women in the fertile age range, 15–44. Of these almost 4.5 million use the National Health Service for family planning measures, with about two-thirds using their local doctor (General Practitioner) and one-third using family planning clinics. According to the General Household Survey in 1993, 72 per cent of women (or their partner) aged 16 to 49 in Great Britain were using a method of contraception. The proportions varied by age group: 76 per cent for those aged 35 to 49, 73 per cent for those aged 20 to 34 and 42 per cent for the 16–19 age group. The main reason for not using a contraceptive among this group was the lack of a sexual relationship. When this factor was taken into account, a large majority of teenagers involved in sexual relationships were using a method of contraception.

Oral contraceptives (the pill) remain the most popular of these methods, especially among the younger age groups, although their relative popularity is declining. The male condom is the next most popular method, and this has grown in popularity. Sterilisation is used by similar numbers of men and women in Great Britain:

around 12 per cent of those in the age group 16–49. In all, 22 per cent of women and 21 per cent of men aged 35 to 49 had undergone sterilisation, compared with 5 per cent of both women and men in the 20–34 age group.

Despite the availability of these measures, an appreciable proportion of pregnancies are ended by legal abortion. Between 1981 and 1992 the number of abortions in Great Britain rose by 34 per cent to 182,800, of which 69 per cent were for women aged 20–34 and 19 per cent for those under 20. Some 19 per cent of the 854,000 conceptions in England and Wales in 1991 were ended by abortion. About 8 per cent of conceptions inside marriage and 34 per cent of conceptions outside marriage ended in abortion in 1991. For teenage conceptions outside marriage the proportion was a little higher, at 37 per cent.

International Comparisons

The crude birth rate in Britain is now above the EU average, estimated at 11.6 in 1991 (see Table 3). The decline in birth rates in the EU partly reflects substantial reductions in crude birth rates in countries such as Greece, Italy and Portugal, from rates in excess of 15 in the early 1970s to much lower levels in the early 1990s.

The pattern of a recent substantial rise in births outside marriage in Britain has occurred elsewhere in the EU, where the overall proportion of births outside marriage is about 20 per cent. Britain has the third highest proportion of births outside marriage in the EU, after Denmark (where nearly half are outside marriage) and France (almost one-third).[12]

[12] Sweden, which joined the EU at the beginning of 1995, also has nearly half of births outside marriage, with a slightly higher proportion than Denmark.

Britain continues to have a much higher teenage fertility rate than most other European countries, the rate in Britain being highest in England and Wales. Teenage fertility rates in many other European countries fell substantially during the 1980s, in contrast to the position in Britain.

Britain also has a higher TPFR than most other European countries, although it is similar to that in developed nations as a whole. Generally, across the industrialised world, fertility rates are continuing to fall to levels below the natural population replacement rate of 2.1 children per woman.

Deaths

In 1993 there were 658,000 deaths in Britain, some 104,000 fewer than the number of births. The number of deaths was similar to the average for the 1970s and 1980s, which fell from 665,000 a year in the 1970s to 657,000 a year in the 1980s. Projected levels are expected to fall further during the next two decades, but then to rise rapidly, reaching over 800,000 a year in the middle of the next century (see p. 14) as people born in the baby boom of the 1960s reach old age.

Death Rates

The mortality rate (the annual number of deaths per 1,000 people—the crude death rate) has steadily improved throughout the 20th century. In the first decade of the century, the crude death rate was above 15 deaths per 1,000 people a year, but by the 1930s it had fallen to below 13. Since then it has fluctuated around 12 deaths per 1,000 people a year, although recently it has been at a lower rate and in 1993 was 11.3 (see Table 11). This lower crude death rate is being achieved despite the growing elderly population.

The causes of the general decline in mortality include better nutrition, rising standards of living, the advance of medical science, the growth and availability of medical facilities, improved health measures, better working conditions, education in personal hygiene and the smaller size of families.

Mortality rates rise with age. They are very low for the young, being 0.2 deaths per 1,000 in 1992 for those aged 1 to 15, with the same rate for males as for females. Thereafter, the rates begin to diverge:

Death rates per 1,000:	Men	Women
16 to 39	1.0	0.5
40 to 64	7.1	4.4
65 to 79	47.0	28.4
80 and above	148.6	111.1

The highest crude death rates in Britain in 1992 were in East Sussex (14.7 per 1,000 people) and the Isle of Wight, and the lowest rates in some counties in the South East and Northern Ireland. These statistics reflect the proportion of elderly people. Age-standardised death rates take the age structure of the population into account. Using these statistics, the death rates are highest in Scotland and the North of England, and lowest in East Anglia and the South West.

Infant Mortality

There have been considerable reductions in infant mortality throughout the 20th century. Three rates are used as a measure of mortality among the very young:

—infant mortality—the number of deaths of infants under one year old per 1,000 live births;

—neonatal mortality—the number of deaths of infants under four weeks old per 1,000 live births; and

Table 11: Death Statistics

	1961	1971	1981	1991	1992	1993
Deaths ('000s)	631.8	645.1	658.0	646.2	634.2	657.7
Mortality rate	12.0	11.5	11.7	11.3	11.0	11.3
Infant mortality rate[a]	22.1	17.9	11.2	7.4	6.6	6.3
Neonatal mortality rate[a]	15.8	12.0	6.7	4.4	4.3	4.2
Perinatal mortality rate[a]	32.7	22.6	12.0	8.1	7.7	9.0
Life expectancy in years at birth:						
Males	67.9	68.8	70.8	73.2	73.6	na
Females	73.8	75.0	76.8	78.7	79.0	na

Sources: OPCS, General Register Offices for Scotland and Northern Ireland, and Government Actuary's Department.

[a] Definitions of the mortality rates are given below. Perinatal mortality statistics are affected by a change in October 1992 in the legal definition of a stillbirth. Previously this related to a baby born dead after 28 completed weeks of gestation or longer, but the new definition covers a baby born dead after 24 completed weeks of gestation or longer.

na = not available.

—perinatal mortality—the number of deaths, including stillbirths, of those under one week old per 1,000 live births and stillbirths.

All three rates have shown a very substantial decline (see Table 11). In 1993 the infant mortality rate was 6.3 deaths per 1,000 live births, the lowest rate ever recorded. It has fallen considerably throughout the 20th century—at the turn of the century the rate stood at 147 and in 1961 it was 22.1. Such dramatic reductions in mortality in the first year after birth reflect in particular the great improvement in pre- and post-natal care.

Within the first year of a child's life, the greatest improvements in mortality rates have been achieved in the first four weeks of life. In 1993 neonatal mortality amounted to 4.2 deaths per 1,000 live births, about 65 per cent of the infant mortality rate. It had declined from a rate of 15.8 deaths per 1,000 live births in 1961.

There has also been a very significant reduction in the perinatal mortality rate, from 32.7 per 1,000 live births and stillbirths in 1961 to 7.7 per 1,000 in 1992. In 1993, on the revised definition (see footnote to Table 11), the rate was 9.0.

Life Expectancy

In 1901 life expectancy at birth was 49 years for men and 52 years for women. Throughout the 20th century, because of the improvements in mortality rates, life expectancy has improved considerably. The expectation of life at birth in 1992 was about 73.6 years for a man and 79 years for a woman. Over the last three decades this has improved by over five years from 67.9 years for a man and 73.8 for a woman (see Table 11). The improvement has been slightly greater for men than for women, since male mortality rates have improved more rapidly. About half of the increase has been achieved by improvements in mortality rates in older age (over 60 years old). Those aged 60 in 1992 could on average expect to have three years more life remaining than they could have expected in 1961: 17.9 years for men and 22.1 years for women. Much of the remaining increase stems from improvements in mortality rates among children, particularly in infant mortality, as considered above.

Main Causes of Death

Major changes in the causes of death since the beginning of the century have included the virtual disappearance of deaths resulting from infectious diseases (notably tuberculosis) and an increase in the proportion of deaths caused by circulatory diseases and cancer. Of the 634,200 deaths in 1992 in Britain, about 46 per cent were due to circulatory diseases, principally ischaemic heart disease and cerebrovascular disease. There has been a reduction in their relative contribution to deaths in recent years from a peak of around 50 per cent in the late 1970s and early 1980s. About 25 per cent of all deaths were due to cancer in 1992, with lung cancer contributing around 6 per cent of deaths. About 11 per cent of all deaths in 1992 were caused by respiratory diseases, with pneumonia accounting for 5 per cent of deaths.

The importance of different diseases varies by age. Circulatory diseases are more significant as the cause of death among the over 65s. For the age group 40–64 circulatory diseases are responsible for more deaths than cancer among men, but among women cancer is much more significant, accounting for over half of all deaths. In 1992 cancer also accounted for a third of deaths among women aged 15 to 39, but about 14 per cent of deaths of men in this age group. For men aged 15 to 39 over half the deaths are as a result of injury or poisoning, compared with 29 per cent for women or girls; this category of deaths only accounts for around 1 per cent of deaths in those aged 65 and over.

Since 1961 there have been a number of causes of death which have seen significant progress in treatment or prevention, more than halving the number of deaths attributable to them. There has been a fivefold reduction in deaths from hypertensive disease, largely owing to improved diagnosis and treatment. Large reductions in the number of deaths from influenza have also been achieved, partly through the introduction of vaccination programmes for the elderly and other 'at-risk' groups. Deaths from congenital abnormalities have fallen considerably, as screening procedures and remedial action have improved, along with greater public awareness.

Other specific causes which have seen improvements in their mortality rates over the three decades include pneumonia and bronchitis and related conditions among men. The number of deaths from bronchitis has fallen substantially since 1984, but those from pneumonia have increased slightly.

Deaths from road vehicle accidents have also declined considerably. In 1993 road accident deaths in Great Britain were 3,814, 10 per cent less than in 1992. This compares with levels of nearly 8,000 a year in the mid-1960s. Great Britain now has one of the lowest rates of road accident deaths of any major industrialised nation. Road accidents still, however, remain the largest single cause of accidental death in Great Britain, accounting for nearly 40 per cent of accidental deaths in 1992.

In spite of the general reduction in mortality rates, there have been some significant increases among particular causes. Causes which have experienced at least a doubling of deaths associated with them in the last three decades since 1961 include cancer of the prostate (men only), diabetes mellitus disease, chronic liver disease and cirrhosis, and lung cancer (women only). However, lung cancer death rates among women are about half those for men, although the death rate among men has fallen in the last 20 years. Although the increase is not as great, deaths from breast cancer among women have continued to increase, accounting for nearly 5 per cent of all female deaths. Drug and alcohol-related deaths have risen in recent years, especially among young people. A total of

10,300 cases of AIDS had been reported by the end of December 1994, of whom 7,000 had died. However, Britain has one of the lowest estimated rates of HIV prevalence in Western Europe.

In 1992 the Government published a White Paper *The Health of the Nation* (see Further Reading), setting out a strategy for improving health in England, with the long-term aim of enabling people to live longer and healthier lives. Targets have been set for improvements in areas such as coronary heart disease, cancers and accidents. Strategies have also been set for Scotland, Wales and Northern Ireland.[13]

Health promotion campaigns are run by the Government on a number of health issues such as cigarette smoking, drugs, AIDS and sensible drinking. For example, on drugs it aims to persuade young people not to take them and to advise parents, teachers and other professionals on how to recognise and combat the problem. The Government is following an active health education policy supported by voluntary agreements with the tobacco industry aimed at reducing the level of smoking further—in 1992 around 29 per cent of adult males and 28 per cent of adult females smoked cigarettes. Cigarette smoking is considered the greatest preventable cause of illness and death in Britain, being associated with around 110,000 premature deaths a year. A three-year national campaign, costing £4 million a year, was started in 1994 and aimed at adult smokers. It is emphasising the dangers of passive smoking and is supported by local authorities to help people to stop smoking. Action is also being taken on a number of other forms of cancer. For example, nationwide screening programmes have been set up for breast cancer for women aged between 50 and 64 and for cervical cancer screening; almost 16,000 women die from breast cancer each year and nearly 1,900 women from cancer of the cervix.

[13] For further information see *Social Welfare* (Aspects of Britain: HMSO, 1995).

International Comparisons

A comparison of crude death rates within Europe shows that Britain has a similar rate to the European average, but is slightly above that for the EU. Its rate was just below that of other EU members such as Denmark and Germany (see Table 3), but above that of countries such as the Irish Republic, the Netherlands and Spain (which have rates below 9 deaths per 1,000 people a year).

Crude death rates are very sensitive to the age structure of the population, however, and it is considered more instructive to compare life expectancy for a clearer indication of differences in mortality rates between countries. Britain's life expectancy at birth of 76 years is slightly above the European average of 75 years, with Greece and Spain having the highest life expectancies, of around 78 years. The range in Western Europe is very similar, ranging from around 75 to 78 years. This is well above the world average, of around 65 years (as estimated by the United Nations). For developed countries the average is 75 years, compared with 62 for developing countries, although Africa has an average as low as 53 years.

Households and Families

The number of households in Britain has increased substantially during the 20th century, from 8 million in 1901 to over 22 million in 1991. Over the last three decades the average rate of increase has been a little under 200,000 a year.

Household Size and Composition

The two main features of the changing pattern of households are the large increase in the number of people living alone and the decline in the size of families. Average household size in Great Britain has fallen substantially, from 4.6 people per household in 1901 to 3.1 in 1961 and to 2.4 in 1993 (see Table 12). Since the General Household Survey started in 1971 the average household size recorded has declined from 2.91 to 2.44 in 1993.

The major component in this steady reduction in average household size has been the large increase in one-person households. Of the 23 million households in Great Britain, about 6 million (27 per cent) are one-person households. Over the last three decades, this has nearly doubled, from 14 per cent in 1961 (see Table 12). This increase has been caused partly by an increase in unmarried (single) people forming households, and partly by a growth in the number of people remaining on their own following the dissolution of a marriage, through separation, divorce or widowhood. In 1991 nearly 32 per cent of households in Greater London were one-person households. In some central London households nearly half of households were one-person, the highest rate being in Kensington and Chelsea (48 per cent). The lowest regional level of one-person households—22.7 per cent—was recorded in Northern Ireland, while in Great Britain the lowest rate by local authority area was in Wokingham (Berkshire)—18.6 per cent.

Table 12: Households in Great Britain

	1961	1971	1981	1991	1993
Number of households (million)	16.2	18.2	19.5	21.9	22.9
Average household size	3.1	2.9	2.7	2.5	2.4
Households of given size as % of all households:					
1 member	14	18	22	27	27
2 members	30	32	32	34	35
3 members	23	19	17	16	16
4 members	18	17	18	16	15
5 members	9	8	7	5	5
6 or more members	7	6	4	2	2

Sources: OPCS and General Register Office for Scotland.

As one-person households have grown in number, so larger households have fallen in number. In 1993 only 7 per cent of all households had five or more people in them, compared with 16 per cent in 1961 and over 40 per cent in 1901. The regional pattern for larger households is fairly similar except that Northern Ireland has a significantly greater number of large households: in 1991, 9.9 per cent of households there consisted of five people, 4.9 per cent of six people and 3 per cent of seven or more people.

Within these changes, the size of the traditional family with children has not fallen, but households without children or with only one parent have increased in number. The average number of dependent children in households with children has remained relatively stable in Great Britain since the early 1980s, at around 1.8 children per household. About 30 per cent of these children were aged under five.

The share of married couple households has fallen from 74 per cent in 1961 to 59 per cent in 1993. There are, however, a similar number of married couples now to those in 1961. Although married couples remain the most common household type, there has been a shift from the traditional nuclear family to a growing emphasis on 'individualisation', which is common to most industrialised nations.

In 1993, according to the General Household Survey, the most common type of household in Great Britain consisted of a married or cohabiting couple with no dependent children (35 per cent of private households). The proportion of households containing the 'traditional' family of a married (or cohabiting) couple with dependent children was 24 per cent, compared with 31 per cent in 1979. Married couples with no children are a lower proportion of households in Northern Ireland than elsewhere in Britain, while conversely households with three or more dependent children represent about 11 per cent of households, more than twice the level in England, Scotland or Wales.

Household size varies according to ethnic group. White households contain fewer people on average than ethnic minority households. For the period 1991–93 the average size of white households was 2.42, while for Indian households it was 3.65 and for black Caribbean households 2.68. The highest average was for Bangladeshi and Pakistani households (around 5), where for both groups there was a particularly high proportion of children.

Families

A declining proportion of people in Great Britain live in the 'traditional' family[14] of a married couple with dependent children— about 41 per cent in 1993, compared with 52 per cent in 1961. During the period 1961 to 1993 there were significant increases in the proportion of people living alone (from 3.9 to 11.1 per cent) and in the proportion living in a family comprising a lone parent with children (from 2.5 to 10.6 per cent).

In Great Britain there were about 9.4 million families with dependent or non-dependent children in 1991, a number which has increased only modestly over the last three decades. Over the same period the number of households without children has grown substantially, from 7.5 million in 1961 to 12.5 million in 1991. The growth in the latter type of household is a major contributing factor to the steady reduction in average household size. Among the relevant factors are the greater life expectancy of adults once their children have left the parental home, and a greater proportion of women going through life without having children. For women in England and Wales born in 1945, 11 per cent were childless at the age of 35, but for women born in 1955 the proportion was nearly double at this age. In 1961, 35 per cent of married couples were living without children, either because they had not yet had children, or they had already left the parental home. By 1991 this figure had steadily risen to 46 per cent.

Families with Dependent Children

The number of families with dependent children[15] has remained relatively stable over the last three decades. In 1991 there were 6.8

[14] A family is a married or cohabiting couple, with or without children, or a lone parent with children. People living alone are not considered a family.
[15] A 'dependent' child is a child under the age of 16 or a non-married person aged 16 to 18 in full-time education and not economically active.

million such families. The composition of these households has changed significantly, however, with a fall in the number of married couples with dependent children. In contrast, the number of cohabiting couples with children grew rapidly in the 1980s, as identified through birth registration information (see p. 81), as did the number of one-parent families.

One-parent Families

In the last five years the number of one-parent families in Great Britain and of dependent children living in these families have risen by about one-third. It is estimated that there were about 1.3 million one-parent families in Great Britain in 1991 (with a provisional figure of 1.4 million for 1992), containing some 2.2 million dependent children (2.3 million in 1992). One-parent families account for a growing proportion of families, having risen from 8.6 per cent of families with dependent children in 1971 to 13.9 per cent by 1986. Subsequently there has been a more rapid rise and by 1993 one-parent families represented 21.8 per cent of families with dependent children.

Lone mothers are much more common than lone fathers. In 1992 provisional estimates indicated that there were 1.28 million one-parent families headed by a lone mother and 120,000 families headed by a lone father, accounting for 19.1 per cent and 1.8 per cent respectively of families with dependent children. Significant changes have occurred in the composition by marital status of one-parent families. The proportions of both lone mothers and fathers who are widowed have fallen substantially, while there has been an increase in the proportion who are divorced. However, among lone mothers single mothers formed the largest group for the first time in 1991, whereas up to the mid-1970s there had been fewer single lone mothers than separated, divorced or widowed lone mothers. There are now nearly 500,000 single lone mothers, over five times the number in 1971. The variations in marital status are reflected in the different age distributions. Lone mothers are generally much younger than lone fathers; in the different age groups, the proportion of lone mothers exceeds that of lone fathers up to the age of 30–34, but in older age groups the proportion of lone fathers is higher. Around 10 per cent of single lone mothers are 15–19, while nearly 40 per cent are aged 20–24.

One-parent families are much more likely to live in metropolitan areas than elsewhere. The highest levels are in inner London boroughs, Manchester, Liverpool and Glasgow; in inner London 37 per cent of families with dependent children were one-parent families, according to the 1991 Census. Five districts—four in London—had levels exceeding 40 per cent, with the highest being in Lambeth (45 per cent). Rural areas generally had many fewer one-parent families. Surrey, Buckinghamshire and the Scottish Islands had the lowest levels, although the district with the lowest proportion was Kincardine and Deeside (8.5 per cent).

Stepfamilies

It is estimated that there were about 500,000 stepfamilies[16] with dependent children in Great Britain in 1991, accounting for about 7 per cent of all families with dependent children. Nearly 5 per cent of families were married couple stepfamilies and 2 per cent cohabiting stepfamilies. These families are much more likely to be based on the natural mother, so that stepfathers are more than three times as common as stepmothers. These stepfamilies contained about

[16] Stepfamilies are married or cohabiting couples with dependent children living in their family, one or more of whom are not the natural children of both partners.

770,000 dependent stepchildren and 280,000 dependent natural children of both partners.

Single Adults

There are now large numbers of unmarried adults in Great Britain, over 11 million in 1991, constituting a quarter of the adult population. This represents a very large growth in numbers of about 50 per cent since 1961, when the single adult population was below 8 million. In England and Wales in 1992, 31 per cent of men aged 16 and over and 23 per cent of women were single (see Table 13).

In England and Wales over half of all single adults are under the age of 25, where they constitute 88 per cent of the population in that age group. About a fifth are 35 or older. In this age group, single adults constitute around 10 per cent or less of the population. A higher proportion than before is in the 25–34 age group, amounting to around 28 per cent of the single adult population. Single adults comprise about 38 per cent of adults in the 25–34 age group, a large proportionate increase on previous decades, reflecting the deferment of marriage (see p. 77).

Among single adults, particularly, there has been an increase in independent living, in lone-parenting and in cohabitation (see p. 79). When young adults do leave the parental home, a higher proportion now leave to live alone or with other single young people rather than to get married. Independence at an earlier age has been made more possible by the greater ease for single a dults to raise finance to purchase their own home, while many more young people are now leaving home as a result of entering full-time higher education.

Table 13: Marital Composition England and Wales

Thousands

	All ages, 16 and over				
	1971	1981	1991	1992	*% 1992*
Males					
Single	4,173	5,013	6,705	6,111	*30.9*
Married	12,522	12,238	11,718	11,672	*59.1*
Divorced	187	611	1,221	1,287	*6.5*
Widowed	682	698	685	684	*3.5*
Females					
Single	3,583	4,114	4,808	4,818	*22.8*
Married	12,566	12,284	11,867	11,823	*56.0*
Divorced	296	828	1,497	1,566	*7.4*
Widowed	2,810	2,939	2,925	2,909	*13.8*

Source: OPCS.

The Parental Home

One of the features of the changes in household and family circum-stances has been a growth in the proportion of men and women in their mid and late twenties who remain in the parental home. This has been attributed partly to the move away from formal marriage. Young men are more likely than young women to remain in the parental home. Around half of men aged 21 to 24 live within the parental home, as against one-third of women. The propor-tions then fall quickly with age, although by the age of 30, 15 per cent of men and 6 per cent of women still remain in the parental home.

People Living Alone

According to the General Household Survey, the proportion of people aged 16 and over in Great Britain who live alone rose from 9 per cent in 1973 to 11 per cent in 1983 and 14 per cent in 1993. Only a small proportion of the younger age groups lived alone in 1993: 4 per cent of the 16–24 age group and 8 per cent of those aged 25 to 44. In the latter age group 10 per cent of men lived alone as opposed to 6 per cent of women.

Overall a higher proportion of women (17 per cent) lived alone, compared with 11 per cent of men, reflecting the much higher proportion of women among the elderly who live alone. Over half of all people living alone are over the age of 65. For those aged 75 and over, 61 per cent of women lived alone in 1993, as against 30 per cent of men. This reflects a greater proportion of women than men in this age group who are widowed, and the higher life expectancy for women. Fewer elderly people are living in their children's homes and fewer are living with other relatives.

Widows and Widowers

About 9 per cent of all adults in Britain were widows or widowers in 1991, totalling over 4 million adults. Some 14 per cent of adult women are widows (3.3 million) compared with only 4 per cent of men (0.8 million) who are widowers, reflecting the greater longevity of women and the tendency for them to marry men older than themselves. There is also a higher rate of remarriage among widowed men and a residual legacy of war widows also remains from the two World Wars. As a consequence, two-thirds of women over 75 years old are widowed, compared with less than a third of men over 75.

One of the results of the large numbers of widowed elderly has been the growth in the number of people living in residential accommodation for the elderly. In 1961 about 100,000 people lived in such accommodation. In 1991 this had nearly trebled to 270,000, with the majority of the increase occurring in the 1980s.

Marriage and Divorce

The prevalence of marriage as a basis of living together is declining across the industrialised world, as it is in Great Britain, particularly among younger generations. Marriage rates have declined, while divorce and cohabitation have grown. Marriage, however, continues to be an important part of the fabric of British society. In 1991, 75 per cent of people in Great Britain were living within that form of family arrangement. Some 60 per cent of adults (16 and over) are married, over 25 million in 1991, representing around 12.6 million married couple households.

The proportion of people living in married couple families has fallen by 7 percentage points from 82 per cent in 1961. This shift has resulted partly from a reduction in the number of first marriages, in favour of remaining single and living independently (see p. 72), lone-parenting (see p. 70), cohabitation and a growth in the rate of divorce (see p. 81), although this is partly offset by increasing numbers of remarriages of divorced people.

Trends in the Number of Marriages

Table 14 shows the general trend in marriages in the period since 1961. There has been a substantial decline in the number of marriages since the late 1960s and early 1970s, when the number of marriages was relatively high, exceeding 450,000 a year. By 1992 the number had fallen to 356,000, 22 per cent lower than in 1971. This decline has been concentrated in the number of first marriages, which fell by 40 per cent between 1971 and 1992, when there were 222,000 first marriages.

The average (mean) age of women at marriage in first marriages has increased, from 22.6 years in England and Wales in 1971 to 25.9 years in 1992. The average (mean) age of men at first marriage is about two years older than that of women. This difference has remained relatively constant and in 1992 the average age for men was 27.9, compared with 24.6 in 1971.

Overall marriage rates have fallen over the last three decades alongside the fall in numbers (see Table 14). In 1992 the marriage rate (the number of people marrying per 1,000 unmarried people aged 16 or over) had fallen to 35.9, compared with 49.4 in 1981. First marriage rates for women have fallen considerably, from 98 marriages a year per 1,000 single women aged 16 and over in England and Wales in 1971 to 47 per 1,000 in 1992. First marriage rates are lower for men, being 37 marriages a year per 1,000 single men aged 16 and over in 1992.

Marriage rates have fallen substantially in the younger age groups. For example, the marriage rates in England and Wales for those aged 20 to 24 declined from 167.7 per 1,000 for men and 246.5 for women in 1971 to 39.2 for men and 70.6 for women in 1992. In 1992 only 1.7 per cent of men and 6.6 per cent of women in their first marriages were aged under 20, as against 10.1 and 31.1 per cent respectively in 1971. The trend for marriages to take place later in life is reflected in lower falls in the marriage rate in the 25–29 and 30–34 age groups. First marriage rates for the age group 35–44 have altered relatively little. For example, the rates in 1992 for England and Wales for men and women in this age group were 33.0 and 31.7 respectively, compared with 33.8 and 30.3 in 1971.

Remarriages

Remarriages are forming a growing proportion of marriages, representing 38 per cent of marriages, compared with 15 per cent in 1961,

Table 14: Marriage and Divorce

	1961	1971	1981	1991	1992
Marriages:					
Number ('000s)	397	459	398	350	356
Marriage rate[a]	na	na	49.4	36.2	35.9
First marriage for both partners ('000s)	340	369	263	222	222
Second or subsequent marriage for one or both partners ('000s)	58	91	135	127	134
Remarriages as % *of all marriages*	*15*	*20*	*34*	*36*	*38*
Divorces:					
Number ('000s)	27	80	156	173	175
Divorce rate[b]	na	na	11.3	13.0	13.2

Sources: OPCS and General Register Offices for Scotland and Northern Ireland.
[a] Number of people marrying per 1,000 unmarried population aged 16 and over.
[b] Number of divorces per 1,000 married population.
na = not available.

primarily reflecting increasing levels of divorce (see p. 81). The number of remarriages rose from 58,000 in 1961 to 134,000 in 1992. In the latter year 75,000 of these involved a remarriage for one of the partners and a first marriage for the other partner, while 59,000 were the second or subsequent marriages for both partners. Over a third of all marriages in 1992 were remarriages where one or both partners had been divorced. However, the remarriage rate for divorced people—the number of remarriages per 1,000 divorced people aged 16 and over—has fallen considerably, for both men and women, to around half the level of 1981 by 1991.

In 1961 remarriages of those widowed exceeded remarriages involving divorced people. This pattern has been reversed and in 1992 in England and Wales about 77,500 divorced women remarried, compared with 8,400 women who had been widowed.

During the 1960s and 1970s the average (mean) age of divorced women and men at remarriage tended to decline, but this trend has been reversed. In England and Wales the average age for divorced women at remarriage rose from 35.1 in 1981 to 37.4 in 1992. On average divorced men are about three years older at remarriage, and in this period the average age of divorced men at remarriage rose from 38.1 to 40.5.

Cohabitation

A feature common to many Western European countries has been an increase in cohabitation—where adults live together as a couple without being legally married. About 18 per cent of non-married men and women aged 16 to 59 in Great Britain were cohabiting in 1993. Between 1979 and 1993 the proportion of non-married women aged 18 to 49 who were cohabiting doubled from 11 to 22 per cent. The highest rates in the early 1980s were among divorced and separated women. Subsequently cohabitation has increased among divorced women and, more particularly, among single women.

Increases in cohabitation have been linked to the trend towards later marriages, especially the first marriage; to an increase in the numbers of people wishing to live together without entering a formal commitment to marriage; and to more people wishing to live together in a trial marriage prior to formalising their relationship. About half of couples getting married for the first time in the late 1980s reported that they had cohabited prior to marriage, compared with only 4 per cent in the 1960s.

The overall proportion of young adults cohabiting increased rapidly during the 1980s. Some 12 per cent of the non-married population was cohabiting in 1986 (11 per cent of males and 13 per cent of females). By 1992–93, 18 per cent of non-married men and women aged 16 to 59 were cohabiting.[17] Those people who have previously been married are more likely than single people to be cohabiting. Among non-married people,[18] divorced people are most likely to cohabit: 37 per cent of divorced men and 23 per cent of divorced women aged 16 to 59 cohabited in 1992–93, while nearly half of all divorced men aged 25 to 34 were cohabiting. A higher proportion of separated men than women cohabited: 24 per cent of separated men and 11 per cent of separated women aged 16 to 59. The equivalent proportions for single people aged 16–59 are 15 per cent and 18 per cent for single men and women respectively. The group least likely to cohabit are widowed people: 8 per cent of widowers and 4 per cent of widows respectively (aged 16 to 59) in 1992–93, partly reflecting the older age of this bereaved group. Cohabiting couples are less likely than married couples to have children living with them. In 1991 about 64 per cent of cohabiting couples had no children living with them, compared with 44 per cent of married couples.

By age the highest rates of cohabitation for non-married men are among those in their early thirties. On the other hand cohabitation by non-married women is highest in the 25–29 age group. Cohabitation rates among non-married men are generally higher than for women in the older age groups, but the reverse is true among the youngest age groups—16–19 and 20–24.

[17] Figures are for 1992 and 1993 combined.
[18] For the purposes of cohabitation, separated people are included in the non-married category.

Cohabitation is highest in the South East (especially in Greater London), East Anglia and the South West. Scotland has a lower rate than in England and Wales, but the lowest rate of cohabitation is in Northern Ireland, where only around 1 per cent of people aged 16 and over were cohabiting in the early 1990s.

There is some evidence that a growing number of non-married relationships are stable. An indication of this can be obtained by examining the address given by parents when registering the birth of a child. In England and Wales in 1992, 55 per cent of births outside marriage were registered to two parents living at the same address, which suggests cohabitation. A further 21 per cent of births outside marriage were registered to joint parents, albeit not at the same address, suggestive of some form of joint parental relationship and responsibility.

Divorce

Divorce has become increasingly significant over the last three decades. Two main legislative changes have facilitated the increase in divorce. In 1971 the Divorce Reform Act of 1969 came into force, making irretrievable breakdown of marriage the sole criterion for a successful divorce petition. This effectively made divorce easier to obtain for those wishing it. In 1984 the Matrimonial and Family Proceedings Act shortened the period of time over which irretrievable breakdown could be established. It allowed divorce to be filed for after one year of marriage. Proposals to reform the divorce laws were contained in a White Paper published in April 1995. Couples would have to wait for at least a year after filing proceedings before they could obtain a divorce, and during this period they would be encouraged to use mediation services.

The number of divorces virtually trebled between 1961 and 1971, reaching 79,600. By 1981 they had almost doubled again to

156,400. Subsequently the number of divorces has continued to grow, but at a much lower rate. However, the number of divorces in 1992 was a record 175,100. The ratio of divorces to marriages in 1992 was 49 per cent, compared with 17 per cent in 1971. Most divorces are granted to women. In England, Wales and Northern Ireland where a divorce is granted to the wife, the most common ground is unreasonable behaviour by the husband. Where a divorce is granted to the husband, the most common ground given is adultery.

The growth in divorce has led to a large increase in the number of divorced people. In England and Wales there were nearly 2.9 million divorced people in 1992, about 7 per cent of those aged 16 and over. The areas with the highest proportions of divorced people in Great Britain in 1991 were in inner London and East Sussex, while the lowest proportion was in the Western Isles. It was estimated that in 1991 there were about 700,000 adults who remain legally married, but are no longer living as a married couple, often prior to legalising the breakdown in the relationship through the process of divorce.

The divorce rate—the number of divorces per 1,000 married people—increased from 2 divorces per 1,000 married people in 1961 to 13.2 in 1992. Within Britain the divorce rate varies considerably, the rates in Scotland and Northern Ireland being lower than in England and Wales. In Northern Ireland, for instance, the divorce rate is only around 4 divorces per 1,000 married people, a third of the average rate for Britain as a whole.

Couples who cohabit before marriage have higher divorce rates than couples who do not. For example, of couples who went through a first marriage in the early 1980s, couples who had cohabited before their marriage had a divorce rate 60 per cent above that of couples who had not lived together before marriage. With the growth in popularity of divorce and subsequent remarriage, a growing pattern of divorce following remarriage has also emerged. In 1961 under 10 per cent of all divorces were of remarried couples. In 1992 the number of couples obtaining a 'decree absolute' in which one or both partners were divorcing for a second or subsequent time accounted for around 26 per cent of all couples divorcing. In general, the likelihood of divorce for a divorced person who remarries is higher than that for a person who marries for the first time at the same age.

With the introduction of the shorter period of irretrievable breakdown required by the 1984 Act, the proportion of marriages lasting less than three years prior to divorce increased from 1.3 per cent in 1981 to 8.9 per cent in 1992. Nearly a quarter of all divorces in 1992 were of marriages which lasted for less than five years. About 27 per cent were of marriages lasting between five and nine years. The average (median) duration of marriage prior to divorce has fallen overall from 12 years in 1971 to 10 years in 1991. The increase in divorce rates has affected all age groups. The highest divorce rates among both men and women are in the 25–29 age group. For England and Wales rates among this age group were 32.9 for men and 31.3 for women (rates per 1,000 married people) in 1991, compared with 5.6 for men and 4.5 for women in the age group of 45 and over. The average age of people at the time of divorce in England and Wales is now about 38.9 for men and 37.4 for women.

Similar large increases in divorce have occurred across much of the industrialised world. Changes in the law in many countries have made it easier for marriages to be dissolved and have relaxed the grounds on which divorce can be granted. Britain had the highest divorce rate of the 12 EU countries in 1992, with a rate of 4.3 per 1,000 population, compared with the overall EU rate of 2.0 per 1,000.

World Population

The world population is estimated by the United Nations to be around 5,660 million. A selection of world population indicators compiled by the UN is given in Table 15.

Britain and many other industrialised countries have experienced lower rates of growth of population in the late 20th century. Some countries, such as the People's Republic of China, have experienced a considerable reduction in growth rates. Fertility rates in areas such as Asia and Latin America have declined considerably.

Nevertheless, a substantial increase in the world's population is forecast. The UN's population projections for the coming 20 years range from 7,100 million to 7,800 million. By 2050 the world population could have reached 10,000 million or higher—the UN's forecasts range from 7,800 million to 12,500 million. Another noticeable trend is the increasing numbers living in urban areas. Nearly three-quarters of the world's population lived in rural areas in 1975, but by the early decades of the 21st century over half of the world's population is forecast to live in cities. Mexico City now has about 15 million inhabitants, while Beijing, Cairo, Seoul and Tokyo each has over 10 million.

UN Conference

The International Conference on Population and Development, held in Cairo in September 1994, was the third UN conference on population, following conferences in 1974 in Bucharest and 1984 in

Table 15: World Population Indicators

	Population (*million*)		Growth rate
	1994	2025[a]	% 1990–95
Europe	512	542	0.3
Africa	682	1,583	2.9
Asia	3,233	4,900	1.8
North America	283	361	1.1
Latin America	458	702	1.8
Oceania	28	41	1.5
World	**5,666**	**8,472**	**1.7**
of which:			
Developed regions	1,238	1,403	0.5
Developing regions	4,428	7,069	2.0

			1990–95		
	Birth rate	Death rate	Infant mort- ality rate	Total period fertility rate	Life expect- ancy
Europe	13	11	10	1.7	75
Africa	43	14	95	6.0	53
Asia	26	8	62	3.2	65
North America	16	9	8	2.0	76
Latin America	26	7	47	3.1	68
Oceania	19	8	22	2.5	73
World	**26**	**9**	**62**	**3.3**	**65**
of which:					
Developed regions	14	10	12	1.9	75
Developing regions	29	9	69	3.6	62

[a] Projected population.   Source: *Social Trends.*

Mexico City. Participants from 180 countries attended the conference, which was the first to deal with population and development issues together. It adopted a 20-year action programme, which did not set demographic targets but focused on the actions needed to allow everyone to make their own choices on childbearing. Reservations on the programme were made by a limited number of countries, for example, on the subject of abortion.

Programme of Action
The programme notes that major shifts in attitude have occurred on subjects such as reproductive health, family planning and population growth. In the next 20 years there will be a further move of rural populations to urban areas, as well as continued high levels of migration between countries. It says that there is emerging global consensus on the need for increased international co-operation on population in the context of sustainable development. Implementation of the goals and objectives of the programme would result in world population growth at levels below the UN's average projection. A selection of some of the main points from the programme is given below.

Fifteen principles are set out. These focus largely on human rights issues as they relate to population and sustainable development. For example, one principle asserts that people are at the centre of concerns for sustainable development and are the most important and valuable resource of a nation, and the right to development is a universal right, and an integral part of fundamental human rights.[19] Another principle says that the family is the basic unit of society. Various forms of the family exist in different social, cultural and political systems. Marriage should be entered into

[19] For more information on human rights see *Human Rights* (Aspects of Britain: HMSO, 1992).

with the free consent of the intending spouses, and husband and wife should be equal partners. Everyone has the right to the highest attainable standard of physical and mental health, and states should take all appropriate measures to ensure universal access to health care services, including those related to reproductive health care (such as family planning and sexual health-care programmes).

The programme states that actions to improve women's access to secure livelihoods and economic resources are needed. Countries should take steps to eliminate inequalities between men and women by establishing mechanisms for women's equal participation. They should also act to eliminate violence and discriminatory practices by employers against women. The programme highlights education as one of the most important means to ensure self-determination for women and therefore urges countries to ensure wide access by girls and women to all levels of education.

Family planning programmes, the programme notes, have contributed to the decline in fertility rates in developing countries, from six to seven children per family in the 1960s to the current level of three to four. The programme sets the tone for a new approach to family planning in the context of better quality comprehensive reproductive health care. It reaffirms the right of all couples and individuals to decide freely and responsibly the number, spacing and timing of their children and to have the information and means to do so. Coercion should have no place in official family planning programmes, the aim of which should be to assist individuals in ensuring that all pregnancies are planned and that all children are wanted. Countries should take steps to meet the family planning needs of their populations as soon as possible and by 2015 should seek to provide universal access to a full range of safe and reliable family planning methods.

Substantial falls in infant mortality in the last two decades are reported, but the programme notes a large gap between infant mortality in developing countries (69 deaths per 1,000 live births) and in developed countries (12 deaths per 1,000 births). It places great importance on the role of primary health care services in reducing further morbidity and mortality in order to guarantee better the survival and health of infants and children, reduce maternal morbidity and mortality, and prevent HIV/AIDS. It notes the deaths of at least 500,000 women a year as a consequence of pregnancy and childbirth—in some countries as many as half of these arise from unsafe abortions. While reflecting the consensus that abortion should not be promoted as a method of family planning, the programme urges countries to act within national laws to reduce deaths and morbidity from unsafe abortion.

By 2015 nearly 56 per cent of the world's population is expected to live in urban areas, compared with just under 45 per cent in 1994. With the rapid growth of urban areas in many parts of the world, the programme emphasises the need to foster a more balanced population distribution by, for example, reducing the inequality between urban and rural areas, fostering environmentally sustainable development of rural areas and of small and medium-sized cities, and managing cities to improve the quality of life of the urban poor.

International migration has risen rapidly. An estimated 100 million people live outside their countries of birth. The majority have migrated on economic grounds, although a significant proportion are refugees or seeking asylum. Governments are urged to address the basic causes of migration, especially those relating to poverty; to encourage more co-operation between sending and receiving countries; to facilitate the reintegration of returning migrants; and to ensure respect for human rights, including those of minorities.

The programme calls on countries to formulate and implement programmes to address the needs of population and development strategies. It affirms that there is a strong consensus on the need for significant additional financial resources for national population programmes in support of sustainable development, including reproductive health and family planning programmes. Governments are urged to strengthen mechanisms for international co-operation. The programme urges the international community to adopt macroeconomic policies for promoting sustained economic growth and sustainable development in developing countries. Although developing countries will continue to provide around two-thirds of the resources needed for their own programmes, international assistance will be required, projected to rise from $5,700 million in 2000 to $7,200 million in 2015.

British Government's View

Speaking at the conference, the Minister for Overseas Development, Baroness Chalker, said that 'the central concern for most of us is the need for urgent action to stabilise the world's population . . . During the last decade we have come to realise that the alleviation of poverty as well as the empowerment of women, their dignity and the need for them to be able to make choices are central issues in population planning.

'We are united by a commitment to enable women and men to access the opportunities that they need to make critical choices—particularly to have children by choice and not chance. We want them to have access to relevant education, to experience safer motherhood and childbirth, and to avoid suffering resulting from sexually transmitted infection, HIV, infertility and sexual violence. In summary, we seek to promote better reproductive health and educational attainment among women, and to involve men, too, in helping to attain this goal.'

There were three substantial challenges:

—to find a way to define reproductive health that is acceptable within different countries;

—for individual countries to examine how they can respond to visions in the programme and to implement those which are appropriate for their people; and

—to help mobilise the resources to meet the costs of implementing 'the Cairo vision' and to ensure that they are well spent.

The Government is involved through its overseas aid programme. It is encouraging private sector groups and non-governmental organisations (NGOs) to establish partnerships with governments and non-governmental groups in developing countries. Through these partnerships it is assisting with planning and implementing relevant health and education services, and supporting relevant social and biomedical research programmes.

In 1990 the Government considered the assistance on population being provided by the Overseas Development Administration (ODA). It decided that the main element of the ODA's population strategy would be to increase the number of women and men who are able to choose how many children they have and when they have children. In 1991 the 'Children by Choice not Chance' initiative was launched. Since 1991, 62 new population and reproductive health projects have been approved for funding, and the ODA's spending on population and reproductive health has increased, reaching £31.6 million in 1993. Two examples of projects are:

—in Kenya, where the ODA has provided nearly £9 million in partnership with the Government of Kenya, the World Bank and bilateral donors to expand the number of places outside the government system where people can get advice and assistance—this has been reflected in higher levels of contraceptive use; and

—in Zimbabwe, where the ODA has agreed with the Government of Zimbabwe to provide a grant of £9 million to help expand sexual and reproductive health care services.

Baroness Chalker said that more resources would be made available by the Government for population activities working in close co-operation with multilateral agencies and the EU. It also expected to provide additional funds to the United Nations Population Fund. In the next two years the Government expected to commit over £100 million to bilateral projects, multilateral organisations and NGOs, representing an increase of 60 per cent on current expenditure.

Appendix: Population and Population Density by County/Region 1993

	Population	Population density (people per sq km)
North	**3,102,300**	**201**
Cleveland	559,500	938
Cumbria	490,200	72
Durham	607,500	250
Northumberland	307,200	61
Tyne and Wear	1,137,900	2,106
Yorkshire and Humberside	**5,014,100**	**325**
Humberside	884,400	252
North Yorkshire	721,800	87
South Yorkshire	1,306,200	838
West Yorkshire	2,101,600	1,033
East Midlands	**4,082,900**	**261**
Derbyshire	950,900	362
Leicestershire	910,300	357
Lincolnshire	601,400	102
Northamptonshire	591,900	250
Nottinghamshire	1,028,400	476

East Anglia	**2,093,900**	**167**
Cambridgeshire	682,600	201
Norfolk	765,100	142
Suffolk	646,200	170
South East	**17,769,400**	**653**
Bedfordshire	539,400	437
Berkshire	763,700	607
Buckinghamshire	651,700	347
East Sussex	722,200	402
Essex	1,560,300	425
Greater London	6,933,000	4,393
Hampshire	1,593,700	422
Hertfordshire	999,700	610
Isle of Wight	124,800	328
Kent	1,539,700	412
Oxfordshire	585,800	225
Surrey	1,037,900	619
West Sussex	717,700	361
South West	**4,768,000**	**200**
Avon	973,300	730
Cornwall and Isles of Scilly	477,000	134
Devon	1,049,200	157
Dorset	667,500	252
Gloucestershire	543,900	205
Somerset	474,100	137
Wiltshire	583,000	168

West Midlands	**5,289,700**	**407**
Hereford and Worcester	694,800	177
Shropshire	413,900	119
Staffordshire	1,053,600	388
Warwickshire	493,600	249
West Midlands (metropolitan county)	2,633,700	2,930
North West	**6,412,400**	**873**
Cheshire	971,900	417
Greater Manchester	2,578,900	2,006
Lancashire	1,420,700	463
Merseyside	1,440,900	2,199
England	**48,532,700**	**372**
Clwyd	415,900	171
Dyfed	351,500	61
Gwent	450,300	327
Gwynedd	240,200	62
Mid Glamorgan	544,300	535
Powys	119,900	24
South Glamorgan	413,200	993
West Glamorgan	371,200	453
Wales	**2,906,500**	**140**
Regions:		
Borders	105,300	23
Central	272,900	104
Dumfries and Galloway	147,900	23
Fife	351,200	269
Grampian	528,100	61

Highland	206,900	8
Lothian	753,900	429
Strathclyde	2,286,800	169
Tayside	395,200	53
Islands areas:		
Orkney	19,760	20
Shetland	22,830	16
Western Isles	29,410	10
Scotland	**5,120,200**	**66**
Northern Ireland	**1,631,800**	**120**
BRITAIN	**58,191,200**	**241**

Sources: OPCS, General Register Office for Scotland and General Register Office for Northern Ireland.

Note: Differences between totals and sums of their component parts are due to rounding.

Addresses

Department of the Environment, 2 Marsham Street, London SW1P 3EB.

Department of the Environment for Northern Ireland, Parliament Buildings, Stormont, Belfast BT4 3SS.

General Register Office for Northern Ireland, Oxford House, 49–55 Chichester Street, Belfast BT1 4HL.

General Register Office for Scotland, New Register House, Edinburgh EH1 3YT.

Government Actuary's Department, 22 Kingsway, London WC2B 6LE.

Office of Population Censuses and Surveys, St Catherine's House, 10 Kingsway, London WC2B 6JP.

Overseas Development Administration, 94 Victoria Street, London SW1E 5JL.

The Scottish Office, St Andrew's House, Edinburgh EH1 3DE.

Welsh Office, Cathays Park, Cardiff CF1 3NQ.

Further Reading

			£
The Health of the Nation: *A Strategy for Health in England.* Cm 1986. ISBN 0 10 119862 0.	HMSO	1992	13.60
Immigration and Nationality. Aspects of Britain. ISBN 0 11 701741 8.	HMSO	1993	4.75
A Social Portrait of Europe. Statistical Office of the European Communities (Eurostat). ISBN 92 826 1747 5.	HMSO	1991	7.00

1991 Census of Population Reports

National Reports:

Report for Great Britain. CEN91 RGB.			
Part 1. ISBN 0 11 691536 6.	HMSO	1993	85.00
Part 2. ISBN 0 11 691526 9.	HMSO	1993	40.00
Report for Scotland.			
Part I. ISBN 0 11 495119 5.	HMSO	1993	65.00
Part II. ISBN 0 11 495120 9.	HMSO	1993	33.00
Report for Wales. CEN91 RW.			
Part 1. ISBN 0 11 691554 4.	HMSO	1993	40.00
Part 2. ISBN 0 11 691562 5.	HMSO	1994	29.00

Reports on Selected Topics:

Children and Young Adults, Great Britain.
CEN91 CYA.* ISBN 0 11 691525 0.   HMSO   1994   47.00

Communal Establishments, Great Britain.
CEN91 CE.* ISBN 0 11 691513 7.   HMSO   1993   33.40

Economic Activity, Great Britain.
CEN91 EA.* ISBN 0 11 691521 8.   HMSO   1994   33.40

Ethnic Group and Country of Birth,
Great Britain. CEN91 EGCB.*
ISBN 0 11 691518 8.   HMSO   1994   45.50

Historical Tables, Great Britain.
CEN91 HT. ISBN 0 11 691509 9.   HMSO   1993   7.60

Household Composition, Great Britain.
CEN91 HC.* ISBN 0 11 691560 9.   HMSO   1993   27.40

Housing and Availability of Cars, Great
Britain. CEN91 HAC.*
ISBN 0 11 691512 9.   HMSO   1993   30.40

Limiting Long-term Illness, Great
Britain. CEN91 LLI.*
ISBN 0 11 691575 3.   HMSO   1993   16.90

Migration, Great Britain. CEN91 MIG.*
Part 1. ISBN 0 11 691519 0.   HMSO   1994   45.40
Part 2. ISBN 0 11 691585 4.   HMSO   1994   12.40

Persons Aged 60 and Over, Great Britain.
CEN91 PEN.* ISBN 0 11 691511 0.   HMSO   1993   16.90

Qualified Manpower, Great Britain.
CEN91 QM.* ISBN 0 11 691586 2.   HMSO   1994   37.90

*Report for England. Regional Health
Authorities.* CEN91 REHRA.

Part 1. ISBN 0 11 691558 7.	HMSO	1993	47.00
Part 2. ISBN 0 11 691559 5.	HMSO	1993	31.00

Sex, Age and Marital Status, Great Britain.
CEN91 SAM.* ISBN 0 11 691508 0.   HMSO   1993   19.00

Topic Monitors published by OPCS are available, price £2, on those subjects marked with an asterisk.

1991 Census County Monitors provide summary statistics for each county in England and Wales. Similar monitors are produced for each region and islands area in Scotland. These are published by the General Register Office for Scotland and are available from HMSO. A two-part County Report published for each county in England and Wales gives detailed statistics from the Census. Similar reports are produced for each region and islands area in Scotland.

Other OPCS Statistics

Published by OPCS and also available on standing order from HMSO.

Abortion Statistics. Series AB.
Birth Statistics. Series FM.
Electoral Statistics. Series EL.
International Migration. Series MN.
Key Population and Vital Statistics. Series PP1/VS.
Marriage and Divorce Statistics. Series FM2.
Mortality Statistics: Cause. Series DH2.
Mortality Statistics: General. Series DH1.
National Population Projections. Series PP2.
Population Estimates. Series PP1.

Other Official Reports and Statistics

Annual Report of the Registrar General for Northern Ireland.	HMSO
Annual Report of the Registrar General for Scotland.	GRO (Scotland)
Control of Immigration: Statistics—United Kingdom.	HMSO
Demographic Statistics.	Statistical Office of the European Communities (Eurostat)
Demographic Yearbook (annual).	United Nations
Family Expenditure Survey Report (annual).	HMSO
General Household Survey (annual).	HMSO
Labour Force Survey Quarterly Bulletin.	Department of Employment
Population Estimates, Scotland.	HMSO
Population Trends.	HMSO Quarterly
Regional Trends (annual).	HMSO
Social Trends (annual).	HMSO
Welsh Social Trends.	Welsh Office

Index

Printed in the UK for HMSO.
Dd.301382, 9/95, C30, 56-6734, 5673.

TITLES IN THE ASPECTS OF BRITAIN SERIES

The Monarchy

Parliament

Parliamentary Elections

Organisation of Political Parties

The British System of Government

History and Functions of Government Departments

The Civil Service

Honours and Titles

Criminal Justice

Britain's Legal Systems

Pressure Groups

Ethnic Minorities

Women in Britain

Human Rights

Religion

Northern Ireland

Wales

Scotland

Immigration and Nationality

Britain and the Commonwealth

Britain and Hong Kong

Britain and Africa

Britain and the Gulf Crisis

Overseas Relations and Defence

Britain and the Falkland Islands

Britain and the Arab-Israeli Conflict

Britain in the European Community

Britain, NATO and European Security

European Union

Britain and the United Nations

Britain and Development Aid

Energy and Natural Resources

Agriculture, Fisheries and Forestry

Transport and Communications

The Aerospace Industry

Telecommunications

Employment

Financial Services

Government and Industry

Planning

Conservation

Housing

Urban Regeneration

Pollution Control

Education

Education After 16

Social Welfare

The Arts

Broadcasting

Sport and Leisure

FORTHCOMING TITLES

Science and Technology